OCKTAIL	PLUM JAM	SPRING ONION	GREEN APPLE	RRY
IG JAM	BLUE DIAMOND SALT	KIWI	RHUBARB	HONEY
ASHED POTATO	CHILLI FLAKES	RANCH	CRANBERRY SAUCE	CAMEMBERT
NNAMON	CORNICHON	RASPBERRY JAM	PEAR	ROSEMARY
IVE	PARMESAN	SAUERKRAUT	HOT PEPPER JELLY	ENDIVE
Y LEAF	MAYONNAISE	BASIL	POPCORN	STILTON
UEBERRY	FIG	PEANUT BUTTER	PECORINO	HABANERO

MW01026647

THE CONDIMENT BOOK

THIS BOOK IS DEDICATED
TO EVERY CURIOUS SOUL. KEEP IT UP!
NO NICHE IS TOO NICHE.

CLAIRE DINHUT

The Condiment Book

A COMPENDIUM OF FLAVOURS

BLOOMSBURY PUBLISHING

LONDON · OXFORD · NEW YORK · NEW DELHI · SYDNEY

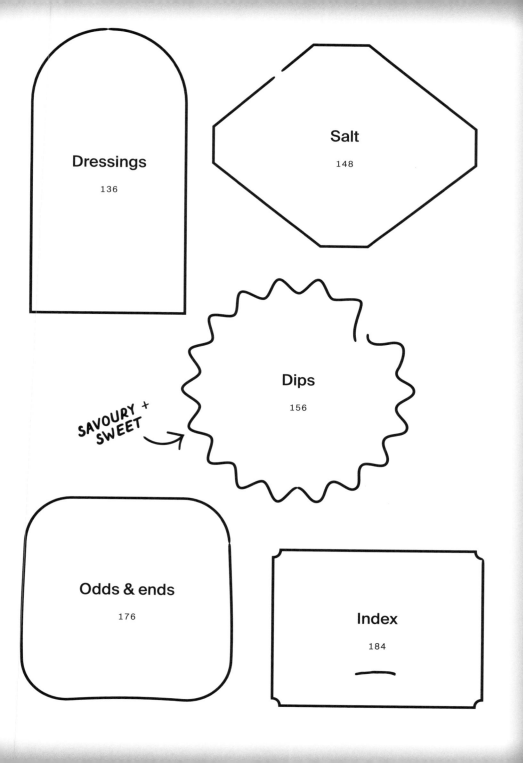

INTRODUCTION

How to use this book

This is not a cookbook.

‼ I repeat, **this is** NOT **a cookbook**.

Instead, think of this book as a **flavour manual**.

I am not a chef, but I consider myself a flavour expert, a flavour adventurer, if you like, and this book is designed to take you on a journey through different condiment lands and categories. And, though I've added recipes, you don't actually need to make any of the condiments in this book. **Shop-bought is always just fine**.

If you do want to try your hand at making them, don't worry, you don't need to be a pro in the kitchen to make condiments. The handful of recipes I've included are intended to inspire you and can be used either as they are, or as a base for leaping off into your own experiments with flavour (one reason why I haven't specified how much any of them make). I hope you do, as condiments both minimise food waste and preserve seasonal flavours when you squirrel them away to relish later.

More importantly, this book contains simple, yet informative, doodles and charts to help you understand flavour pairings, which themselves will provide a gateway to your own journey, as you follow your own path of culinary curiosity.

Starting off simple, we have **Classics**: ketchup, mayo, mustard and butter. From here, we jump to **Spicy** condiments such as hot sauce and scrumptious candied jalapeño bites. To counteract the heat, we'll then dive into some **Fruit in jars**: jam, jelly and – my personal favourite sweet-yet-acid surprise – chutney. Then we'll move on to **Pickles & ferments**, **Dressings & oils**, **Salt**, then **Dips** both savoury and sweet.

And yes, I keep writing 'we' because I will be there with you the entire time, holding your hand as we explore the wacky world of condiments. Be prepared for us to be mutually bonded by unique combinations that had never occurred to us before, but which – from now on – we won't ever be able to live without.

Oh, but what will I eat with all these condiments, Claire? Don't worry, dispersed through the book are a sprinkling of my most-loved **Condiment Companions** (vehicles, in layman's terms), as well as my favourite pairings for all sorts of condiments, some standard, but most pretty unusual and, hopefully, thought-provoking.

Again, **this is** NOT **a cookbook**, just our personal diary of fun eats to tantalise our tastebuds and keep life exciting.

My top 12 condiment essentials

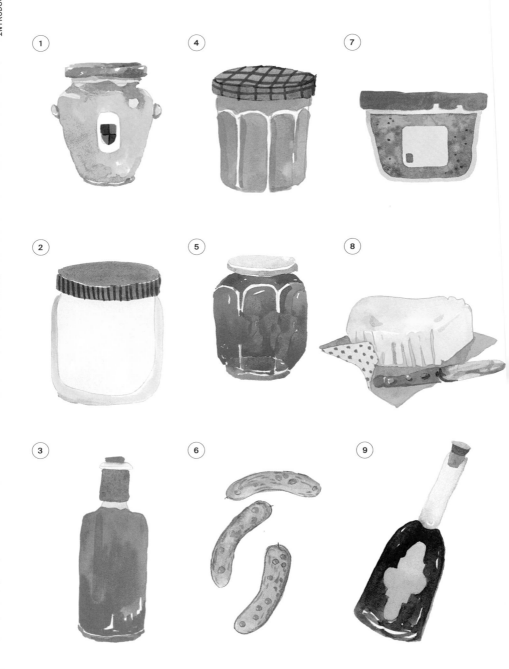

1

4

7

2

5

8

3

6

9

1 MUSTARD

American yellow mustard, **Dijon**, grainy Dijon

2 MAYONNAISE

Dijonnaise, Japanese mayo, regular mayo

3 SPICY KICK

Any hot sauce (mild to hot), my genius **Candied jalapeño bites** (see page 60), chilli crisp, Mexican tomatillo salsa verde

4 SOMETHING FRUITY

Candied fruit, **jam**, jelly

5 CHUTNEY

Ploughman's pickle, spicy mango chutney

6 PICKLES

Cornichons, gherkins, pickled ginger, pickled onions

7 SOY-BASED CONDIMENTS

Miso, ponzu, **soy sauce**

8 FAT

Butter, ghee, lard, olive oil

9 VINEGAR

Apple cider vinegar (ACV), **balsamic vinegar**, sherry vinegar, white or red wine vinegar

10 SALT

Fleur de sel, kosher, Maldon, pink Himalayan, sel gris

11 SPICES

Cinnamon, cloves, juniper berries, mustard seeds, star anise

12 HERBS

Basil, coriander, dill, oregano, parsley

CHOOSE YOUR FIGHTER

I'VE HIGHLIGHTED MY ABSOLUTE FAVOURITES IN EACH CATEGORY. IF I HAD TO PICK JUST ONE (WHICH WOULD HONESTLY BE DEVASTATING)

This book is about curiosity. What excites our tastebuds? How can we evoke feelings with every bite we take? How can we maximise flavour through mindful pairings and bold combinations? How can we travel the world while sitting at a table? The purpose of this book is to help you train your palate to experience different – often unexpected – mixtures of flavour, suited to your personal taste receptors.

The rise in food culture and resulting culinary curiosity has become an international phenomenon, with people around the world more open than ever to discovering new flavours and having authentic food experiences. Food has even become a driver of international tourism. Of course, every culture has foods and recipes they call their own, but how is a sense of place imparted when we all start with the same basic ingredients? Let's take chicken as a global staple. What differentiates one culture's chicken dishes from another is the addition of flavour through condiments – sauces, spices, seasonings, dressings – and with just a single forkful, chopstickful or pinch, we've tasted centuries, if not millennia, of culinary history.

Now, you may be asking yourself, what exactly is a condiment? The word derives from the Latin verb *condire*, which means 'to preserve, pickle, season, spice, render pleasant or **enhance flavour**'. A *condimentum* itself in the Roman Empire would have been any sauce, seasoning, spice, relish or sweetener. That extra cherry on top, that last delectable addition that isn't really needed but most certainly completes a dish. It's the flavour combination your tastebuds will remember and which leaves you wanting more, craving that exact flavour for days and – in some happy cases – for a lifetime.

Let's go back to that **enhance flavour** part, as it is the core message of this book. Taste is not flavour; rather, taste is a subset of flavour. 'Taste' is the element of flavour that has to do with your tastebuds, the physical sensors on your tongue. 'Flavour', however, though it includes what is happening on your tongue, also encompasses what is going on in your mind and imagination. You can find something flavoursome because of scent, colour, nostalgia and more. As famously evidenced in Marcel Proust's *In Search of Lost Time*, flavour evokes involuntary memories. With one bite of a madeleine, Proust was unexpectedly transported to his childhood; the past flooded back.

Condiments are key to such vivid experiences: they are the flavour enhancers and flavour creators in a dish and, therefore, they are often what fire up the subconscious and overwhelm us with feelings.

Though many do have health benefits, condiments are unnecessary for nutrition. We can exist and nourish ourselves without them. But why would we? They are vital for flavour, pleasure and the passing-on of tradition. On a micro level, they're what makes a meal memorable; on a macro scale, they define a culture and its cuisine.

Why should you care what I say?

Luckily for me, I was raised in a family that celebrated food, seasonal eating and local ingredients, a product of my mother's Greek heritage, my father's French upbringing and the melting pot of culinary offerings that is the US. While many children have memories based on play, mine are based on flavour.

In France, everyone jams, cans, conserves, preserves, pickles and more. Regardless of whose kitchen you step into, you'll find their own signature jar and, believe me, it will get used. In French bookshops, half the cookery section is composed of conserving and preserving manuals: it's completely ordinary. So, while I'm now known as Condiment Claire online, I'm really just French.

This book is definitely skewed towards a more Western palate, purely because of where – and the way in which – I was raised. Though we will be exploring flavours from all over the world, most of my early flavour memories were created in the Mediterranean cultures of France, Italy and Greece. However, since I grew up primarily in LA, I also have the immense privilege of that state's signature Mexican and Japanese flavours evoking a deep-rooted nostalgic and comforting feeling in me. So, in this book, you will find recipes influenced by my heritage, others that represent my favourite cultural mish-mashes, as well as condiments that I have learned to make via friends and wellwishers from other cultures (hello miso).

But before we head into our flavour deep-dive, let's discuss the more straightforward nature of taste.

ALL YOU NEED TO REMEMBER IS THAT CONDIMENTS = FLAVOUR

Taste

Taste triggers tastebuds. These little dots on your tongue, which scientists call *papillae*, are connected to your brain and activate depending on what you put into your mouth. We learn about them in kindergarten with the help of a 'taste map' and sense them with every bite we take. They've been in our mouths since birth, they are responsible for how we taste our food (and condiments, of course).

Years ago, chemosensory scientists discovered that these five 'areas' on our tongues, each relating to a separate flavour, are actually fictitious. Rather, taste receptors are evenly scattered all over the surface of our tongues... but that's no fun, is it?

As humans, we always pick favourites, so we tend to gravitate towards two or three of the five tastes. Do you prefer savoury or sweet foods? Personally, I'm a keen advocate of sour and umami tastes.

Taste is what the body feels when 'action potentials' – the results of sensory stimuli – are triggered. These provoke the taste area of the brain, which sends the body a cue to release enzymes, gastric juices and all that good stuff that allows us to digest food.

Overall, humans are born with up to 10,000 tastebuds. Not only do these taste receptors regenerate naturally every ten days or so, but they also decline with age, so **you will taste foods differently as you get older**. Younger people, with more tastebuds, have a heightened sense of taste. This may be why you hated blue cheese as a child and now quite enjoy its pungency: fewer receptors translate to higher palatability. Further, olfactory fibres in the nose decline with age. Since these work alongside tastebuds to discern flavour, when those nasal fibres weaken, the entire system is affected.

(THEY'RE NOT THE SAME THING!)

Flavour vs taste

We use the terms 'flavour' and 'taste' interchangeably, but they are entirely distinct from one another. Simply put, taste is the basic feeling on the tongue that connects our tastebuds to our brain. It is comprised of five sensations: bitter, salty, sour, sweet and umami. Flavour, on the other hand, is a much more convoluted sensation. It's an immersive whole-body-and-mind feeling that embraces both conscious and subconscious, real and remembered.

Taste map

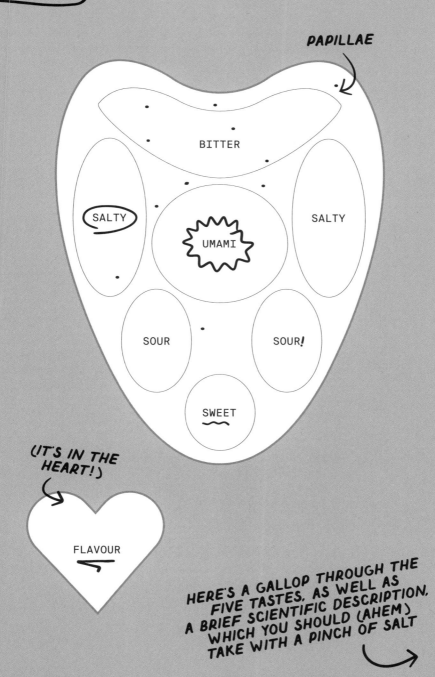

PAPILLAE

BITTER

SALTY

SALTY

UMAMI

SOUR

SOUR!

SWEET

(IT'S IN THE HEART!)

FLAVOUR

HERE'S A GALLOP THROUGH THE FIVE TASTES, AS WELL AS A BRIEF SCIENTIFIC DESCRIPTION, WHICH YOU SHOULD (AHEM) TAKE WITH A PINCH OF SALT

Bitter

The term 'bitter' has negative connotations and is commonly used to describe an acrimonious or spiteful person, but – as a taste – I find it a fantastic gateway to life-changing and memorable combinations. Yes, it is certainly on the harsher side, but it marries well with sweet and salty tastes. Cacao, coffee, juniper, hops, citrus zests, olives and dark leafy greens such as kale all taste bitter. On their own, they are definitely astringent, but paired with another taste, they can contribute to a match made in flavour paradise. Cacao with sugar? Coffee and a splash of milk? Campari topped up with sweet sparkling wine? Sign me up.

Scientists once believed a bitter taste was a warning of harmful poisonous or rotting food, a taste that signalled to the brain to spit it out. However, more recent studies have shown that we detect that a food is bitter due to a compound we still know nothing about.

Salty

Scientifically speaking, the taste of salt is the taste of positive sodium ions such as sodium chloride – NaCl – sparking an action potential. Since salt itself is the primary marker of salty taste, anything which contains the condiment (yes, salt is a condiment) will trigger its taste, chips, pizza and crisps included.

My favourite way to pair salty foods is with their directly opposing taste: sweet. You can elevate a basic chocolate chip cookie by tossing on sea salt flakes, jazz up watermelon with feta chunks, or slather maple syrup on your crispy bacon for the perfect morning combo.

Sour

Simply put, the taste of acid! As with the connection above between saltiness and sodium, sourness is connected to hydrogen ions. The more sour something is, the more hydrogen ions there are in it.

Lemons, vinegar, passion fruit and sauerkraut all fall under this category. Delicious and mouth-puckering, sour foods are explosive sensory phenomena. Adding a sweet flavour will reduce the sour taste, which is why you'll commonly see duos such as rhubarb and strawberry paired up, or lemon and honey, or tamarind and date.

Sweet

Oh, that sweet tip-of-the-tongue feeling. Few moments beat the rush triggered by an afternoon slice of chocolate cake, a luscious scoop of ice cream on a sweltering summer's day, or a handful of sweets from a rustling bag in the cinema.

While the taste of sweetness comes from sugars or alcohols – such as glycerol and anethol – hitting the tongue, something can taste sweet without containing any sugars. Just think of cinnamon, stevia or liquorice.

Umami

The most recent addition to the taste bunch; scientists only discovered this fifth taste receptor in the 1990s. It encapsulates all taste that is 'appetitive'. The word umami itself comes from a Japanese term that is directly translated as 'good flavour', or 'the pure essence of deliciousness'. With just one umami nibble, you immediately want more.

Technically, the 'taste' of umami is the taste of glutamate, an amino acid that is a key building block of protein. MSG, soy sauce, fermented foods, meat, anchovies, mushrooms, salmon, dashi and more all fall under this umbrella. It's my all-time favourite taste, as it's complete on its own, yet can still be balanced by the other four...

- Umami and salty: mushrooms and well-seasoned steak

- Umami and sweet: soy sauce and maple syrup

- Umami and bitter: miso and Brussels sprouts

- Umami and sour: ponzu sauce (a soy sauce and citrus combo)

SEE PAGE 134 FOR HOMEMADE PONZU

Taste connections

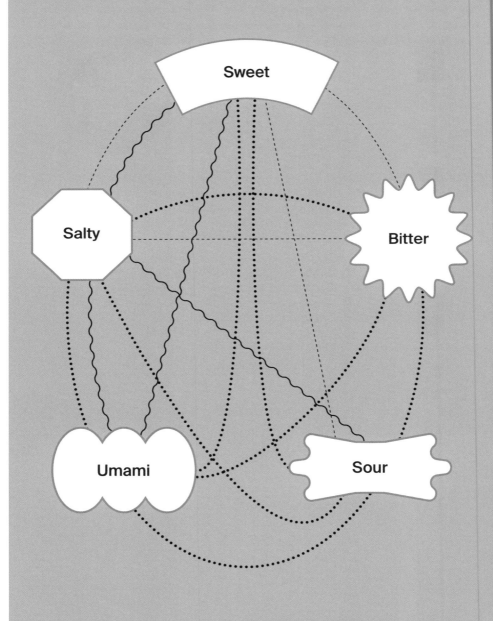

ENHANCES ∿∿∿∿∿∿∿

REDUCES --------

BALANCES •••••••••••••••••

Flavour

As we've seen, though it's a vast and complex subject, taste is simply a subset of flavour. So let's get on to the fun part. Flavour is where we derive the sensation of culinary pleasure and in which condiments play a central role. The purpose of this book is to teach you how to maximise flavour and experiment with creating flavour combinations that will forever excite your palate. But before you can do this, you should probably understand exactly what flavour is.

While taste only happens in your mouth, **flavour is a full-body experience**, primarily due to the inclusion of scent. While we can perceive five distinctive tastes – at least, that we know of as I write – we are able to discern nearly 10,000 aromas. Odour plays an enormous part in how our bodies react to eating food. Sniffing, or 'orthonasal olfaction' in non-layman's terms, does not have anything to do with flavour. Rather, flavour is sensed through retronasal olfaction, which is scent coming through the back of the mouth. With every exhalation, the back of your throat is able to taste-smell all of those (hopefully delicious) stimuli within your mouth.

Just think about when you have a blocked-up nose: everything is so... meh. You can feel the texture of the food you're eating, but otherwise it gives off beige and bland energy. So you may be surprised to learn that loss of smell, or anosmia, does not affect the ability to sense taste whatsoever. Even if you feel as though you can't 'taste' anything when you're unwell, you actually can, you just can't smell it! That proves how important smell is in comparison to taste when it comes to flavour and, ultimately, to pleasure.

Enough about smell, let's get into the simpler components of flavour such as sound and colour. These are relatively straightforward: the sound of a coffee machine whirring, of butter sizzling, of the soft-slap whipping of cream... all these noises will trigger your desire to eat, so flavour is already beginning to develop before you have taken a single bite. **Sound can also change your perception of taste**. Loud noises, such as in a busy and cramped restaurant, can even suppress the feeling of sweetness as well as heighten the sensation of umami!

Since flavour is in part psychological, it shouldn't surprise us that colour plays a crucial role in its perception. A grey-green bean probably won't be as appealing to you as its bright green sister. Sure, this could be to do with cooking technique, but if you go to bite into something with a funky colour, you probably won't have high expectations. The psychological effect of colour creates an assumption of texture and taste that influences the body's eventual sensation of flavour.

All this leads the eater to judge the food, not taste it.

 WILD

What kind of eater are you?

As I always say, food is an individual journey. Food scientists argue that there are four types of eaters in the world: chewers, smooshers, suckers and crunchers. Depending on how you eat, you will experience different food textures and, thus, different flavour.

WHICH ONE ARE YOU?

CHEWERS

These eaters take a long time over their food, as they enjoy the sensation of fullness in their mouth. Ideally, their food doesn't break down quickly and is able to provide them with chewy satisfaction for as long as possible.

SMOOSHERS

A type who likes to use their tongue and palate more to eat. Unlike crunchers and chewers, smooshers tend to break down their food into a smooth texture and spread it throughout their mouth. They are also slow eaters.

SUCKERS

Another tribe of slow eaters, this group suck their food for as long as possible to extract maximum flavour before swallowing. As with crunchers, their ideal food is hard, but only so that they can keep it in their mouths for as long as possible.

CRUNCHERS

A group who bite on their foods forcefully and usually tend to eat quickly. They like to crunch down aggressively, even on soft foods such as ice cream and yogurt.

I'M MOST DEFINITELY A CRUNCHER

THIS MAY DETERMINE WHICH FLAVOURS YOU ENJOY + WHICH STAND OUT TO YOU DUE TO THEIR TEXTURE

Flavour is sensed once food breaks down in your mouth and releases chemicals, so it's only after chewing for a little while that you can feel any dispersed sensation, and thus flavour. Therefore, depending on whether you're a chewer, smoosher, sucker or cruncher, you will literally experience the same food in a different way. Additionally, the texture of a certain food determines how quickly you receive those sensations. Take chewing gum, for example: with every chew you can taste flavour, as gum's whole *raison d'être* is elongated mastication. But a swig of orange juice – with its shock of tastebud-wakening citrus-sour – is delivered to the mouth, then vanishes in a rollercoaster-ride instant.

Texture also affects mouthfeel. Most people who think mayonnaise is gross explain that this is because of its gloopy texture. Humans have created learned connections between food texture and flavour, so if you eat something and you hate its mouthfeel, you're definitely not going to appreciate its flavour.

Last but certainly not least is the fact that **memory** plays a giant role in flavour. I feel extremely passionately about this. Both good and bad memories will determine how you think about a certain food or meal. Take my dad, for example: he cannot stand the 'flavour' of soup. After some digging, I've come to realise that this is because anything hot and liquid reminds him of difficult winters growing up poor in the French countryside. Why would he want to feel that way ever again? On a more positive note, he loves fruit. This, he'll admit, is because it reminds him of the special treats his parents could afford once in a while, or that he was able to pick from trees at his grandparents' farm at weekends.

Similarly, to me, oysters are some of the most delicious bites in the world. Briny and fresh, they remind me of the most joyful time of my year while I was growing up: holidays to see my family in France during the winter. The combined tastes of vinegar, shallot and a squeeze of lemon juice on a tiny Fine de Claire oyster transport me back to that French Christmas table, surrounded by my loved ones. I wasn't allowed a raw oyster until I was three and, even then, I only got half, as my parents were reluctant to let me challenge my developing digestive system with raw bivalves, but I revelled in even that small bite.

Such food histories are, of course, unique to each of us, and this book will allow you to explore your own individual flavour path. How can any of us share another's favourite flavours without having lived their exact life?

Now that's settled, let's get deep into each arena of condiments, every kitchen shelf of flavours, on **a quest for some new lifetime loves**. I can guarantee there will be many new combinations and surprising discoveries hidden in these pages that are perfectly tailored to you and your personal flavour preferences...

CLASSICS

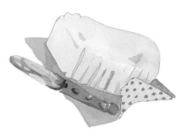

HALL OF FAME CONDIMENTS:
KETCHUP, MAYO,
MUSTARD + BUTTER →

When I think of classic condiments, ketchup, mayonnaise and mustard immediately spring to mind. You'll often see one served alongside the other, they're frequently a trio. There's a good reason for that: the acidity in mustard works with the creaminess of mayonnaise and the sweetness of ketchup to perform choreography on your tastebuds during each bite, and the applause lingers even after swallowing.

But how could I **NOT** include butter in this Classics chapter? Especially considering I have posted videos of myself on the internet tasting it by the chunkful. I simply **must** maintain my butter fan-girl status. It would be rude not to. Also, I have solid proof (literally) that it is a condiment. A condiment is something added, that little extra topping, right? When you make toast and add jam, you consider jam as a condiment, correct? Same goes for butter. While it may melt if you spread it on a scrumptious toasty slice of bread, it's still there.

While these four condiments have obvious pairings, I want you to **think BIGGER.** What do you love about the combination of ketchup and chips? Is it the sweet flavour of the sauce mixed with the salty chips? In that case, try ketchup with fermented vegetables. Or is it the glossy ketchup texture contrasting with the starch from the potato? Try it with roast parsnips. There are simply no restrictions in the world of condiments: it's just you, your tastebuds and lots of creativity.

Now that you're in the right mindset, let's explore the world of these classic condiments, which most of us always have to hand. Hopefully, you will learn something new about your flavour preferences and be able to make as many flavour combinations as you wish, from the comfort of your own kitchen. The chart opposite will help you narrow down your individual top flavour areas.

IT'S WFH FLAVOUR UNIVERSITY

The condiment super league

Asking people what their top three favourite condiments are can be an ice-breaker, or a friend (and enemy) maker. Play it at work, in a coffee shop, at the pub... Let's just say you'll be remembered, so be sure to ask, then run away. Or try the non-confrontational version below, with just you and a pen.

BUTTER

KETCHUP

MUSTARD

MAYONNAISE

FILL IN YOUR ALL STAR PLAYERS

GHERKINS

KIMCHI

CAESAR

RANCH

YOUR PERSONAL CONDIMENT CHAMPION

HOT SAUCE

SOY SAUCE

JAM

CHUTNEY

SALT

PEANUT BUTTER

HONEY

LEMON CURD

KETCHUP

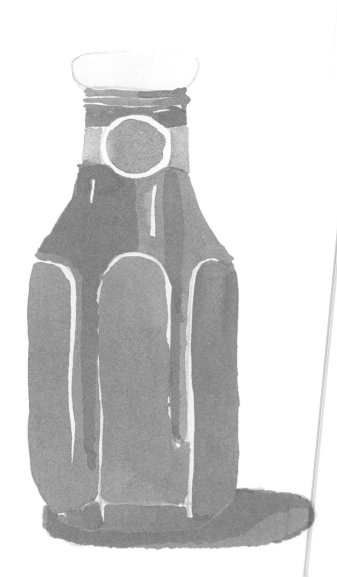

The easiest way to describe ketchup is as a spiced and vinegared purée of vegetables, used as a relish. Though we usually picture it as red and tomatoey, it can be made from diverse vegetables and its ingredient history and journey are both vast. It's a workhorse – a dutiful staple of any kitchen – and I refuse to judge anyone's ketchup usage. I will always need it on a burger, hotdog or chips, but you may use it with eggs, rice, even carrot sticks if that's what your heart desires.

Though it's sometimes looked down upon as childish, ketchup is one of the few condiments that encapsulates **all five core tastes**, which is quite rare. It is sweet, salty, bitter, sour and umami all at the same time. Because of this multitude of taste notes, it is used as a mother sauce in many other condiments: barbecue, spicy Korean fried chicken and thousand island, to name just three.

History of ketchup

Today, when we think of ketchup, we think of the tangy-sweet tomato sauce, but you might be surprised to know that the first ketchup wasn't made from tomatoes. Originally called *kê-tsiap* in Hokkien Chinese, the original 'ketchup' was most likely made from fermented fish. China's textile and spice trade with South East Asia in the 17th century brought this delectable, mouth-puckering sauce to the attention of British and Dutch merchants and they simply had to recreate it back home. And yet the first English ketchup recipes, recorded as early as 1732, were still not made from tomatoes, but rather from other savoury, umami-rich ingredients such as mushrooms and walnuts. As time passed, the passion for ketchup in Europe only grew. In the 18th century – which I like to think of as the Golden Age of Ketchup – diverse recipes for ketchups appeared in cookbooks, made from lemons, celery, plums, peaches, oysters, anchovies and more.

The first tomato ketchup recipe appeared nearly a century later, in 1812 in the United States, which is perhaps why, for Americans, there really is only one ketchup. We can credit James Mease, a Philadelphia scientist, for developing the OG. He single-handedly changed the course of the condiment's trajectory, as back then tomatoes were widely believed to be poisonous. (This mistaken idea came about because plates were commonly made with lead. Tomato juices would leach into the plates they were served on and, due to their high acidity, cause lead poisoning in the unfortunate diners.) Mease created a tasty sauce using these 'love apples' (tomatoes were also thought to have aphrodisiac powers). During the mid-1850s, tomatoes even began to be recommended by medical professionals to **strengthen the body**, which led to the sauce's increased success.

Tomato ketchup became very popular, but unfortunately it went off quickly. Most condiments and sauces were, at the time, kept in coloured vessels, to make it hard for customers to determine their freshness.

Now, please welcome another very important man whose name is synonymous with the condiment today: Mr Henry J Heinz. As an entrepreneur, he was extremely focused on customer trust, so, in the late 1800s, he made the ingenious addition to tomato ketchup of vinegar, a natural preservative, allowing him to package the vibrant red sauce in clear glass bottles. This accomplished two things at once: it instilled customer trust and increased the appetite for the beautifully coloured sauce. The colour red has an immense and measurable physical effect on the brain, triggering its reward system, which may well have helped in making tomato ketchup so popular. To further strengthen brand loyalty, in 1906 Heinz launched a preservative-free ketchup which, though higher priced than the standard varieties on the market, gained a massive following.

And now on to the heroine of ketchup history, Maria Orosa, a chemist of Filipino origin who studied in the United States in the early 1900s. Upon returning to her native country, she dedicated herself both to food science and to limiting her country's reliance on imports. Tomato ketchup had become popular in the Philippines during the American occupation in the late 1800s. Since tomatoes were not native to the Philippines, and were a major import, Orosa used her savvy to recreate the flavour and viscosity of American ketchup without using them. Please give a round of applause to bananas. Though a bit more viscous than standard tomato ketchup, Orosa managed to concoct a banana ketchup to entice her countrymen of the same taste, texture and colour as the tomato variety (with a bit of help from food colouring), but using the bountiful fruits of their islands. Today, **banana ketchup** is a staple in the Philippines and a cultural flavour marker. Filipino households rely on the condiment and you will rarely find any without it.

To wrap this up, the sweet taste of ketchup, alongside its umami notes, simply can't help but be completely addictive. (Especially to the denizens of Canada and Finland, who share the title of the world's top ketchup consumers.) Just pity its young fans in France, where ketchup is banned in school cafeterias unless it is served with French fries, to limit sugar consumption and encourage traditional Gallic cuisine.

Ketchup around the world

Ketchup is still found in many different forms beyond tomato. Each variety is specifically appreciated because of how well it pairs with the other flavours of a particular region.

This list is of course not exhaustive, but, as with the other maps sprinkled through these pages, I hope it gives a broad brush overview into condiment preferences (and oddities) all over the globe.

And perhaps some of the ways in which condiments are used and enjoyed in different cultures worldwide might spark some ideas and kitchen experiments in many of us, too.

1 CHINA

The first ever ketchup: fish ketchup

2 USA

James Mease was credited with the first tomato ketchup recipe, in 1812

3 PHILIPPINES

Maria Orosa's banana ketchup took the nation by storm

4 GERMANY

Curry ketchup, vital for their beloved sausages

5 JAMAICA

Jerk ketchup perks up the palate

6 JAPAN

Tonkatsu sauce, made with ketchup, is used on fried and breaded items

7 ENGLAND

Mushroom ketchup was the ketchup condiment of choice before tomatoes arrived

8 THAILAND

Ketchup-flavoured potato chips are big

9 POLAND, LEBANON, TRINIDAD

All these nations like ketchup with pizza

10 CANADA

Ketchup cake (yes, really, a sweet cake made from ketchup) is a thing here

11 SWEDEN

Ketchup-as-pasta sauce is common

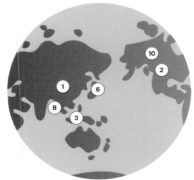

How to make ketchup

I'll come clean: I don't really believe in making my own ketchup when shop-bought is so abundant and delicious, but should you run out entirely while hosting a barbecue, you will now be prepared.

I always like using a concentrated tomato purée here, as I find it gives the most pungent base flavour to ketchup: sweet with herbaceous depth. When using concentrate, there is no need for additional sugar, as it is so reduced that it almost tastes caramelised (another benefit to making your own, as most shop-bought ketchup is packed with unexpected amounts of sugar).

Any time I see the open flame of a barbecue, I think of how I could be using ketchup to maximise flavour. As a mother sauce and a key ingredient in a great barbecue sauce, it's fantastic slathered on a piece of meat or a vegetable before tossing it on the grill. A ketchup glaze provides much of that glossy, sweet coating that leaves you with sticky bits on your face after devouring a succulent pork spare rib.

WHAT YOU NEED

200g concentrated tomato purée
80ml apple cider vinegar (ACV)
½ tsp onion powder, or granules
¼ tsp garlic paste
⅛ tsp ground cumin
salt and pepper
bowl

WHAT TO DO **1** Combine all the ingredients in the bowl, season well and mix. As easy as that! Please cover and keep any homemade ketchup in the fridge, where it should last for about 1 week.

Due to its vast taste profile – ranging from salty to umami – ketchup can and should be used more frequently than it is. Just remember that ketchup has a warm and sweet flavour profile, so counterbalance it with a salty, cold or crispy match.

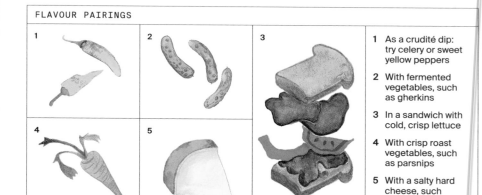

FLAVOUR PAIRINGS

1

2

3

4

5

1 As a crudité dip: try celery or sweet yellow peppers

2 With fermented vegetables, such as gherkins

3 In a sandwich with cold, crisp lettuce

4 With crisp roast vegetables, such as parsnips

5 With a salty hard cheese, such as pecorino

Fun ketchups

These **should** use homemade ketchup as the base. You could technically mix in the add-ins to a shop-bought ketchup, but I find that the sauce's texture is nicer, and its flavour profile more rounded, when you use the ketchup recipe opposite.

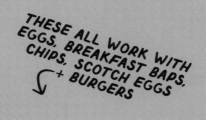

THESE ALL WORK WITH EGGS, BREAKFAST BAPS, CHIPS, SCOTCH EGGS + BURGERS

Bloody Mary ketchup, or hair-of-the-dogchup

Add ¼ tsp celery salt, 1 tsp horseradish, the juice of ½ lemon, ½ tsp hot sauce (*ideally red, to keep the colour bright*) and 1½ tsp Worcestershire sauce

'Not puttanesca' ketchup

Before meaning 'prostitute', *puttana* meant 'stinky' in Italian. You're basically just doing the linguistic origin justice by adding as much garlic and anchovy as your body can handle.

Add 2 tbsp drained and chopped capers in brine, ½ tsp caper juice from the jar, 2 tbsp drained chopped black olives in brine (*such as Kalamata*), ½ tsp olive brine, 1 tsp anchovy paste (*or 2–3 chopped anchovies*), ½ tsp finely chopped or grated garlic (*yes add more garlic to the base recipe, trust me on this*), 1–2 tbsp chopped parsley leaves and 1 tsp chilli flakes (*optional but delicious*)

Spicy Korean ketchup

Add 1 tsp gochujang, 1 tsp finely chopped or grated garlic, 1 tsp fish sauce and ¼ tsp shrimp paste

NOW ON TO THE LOVE-IT-OR-HATE-IT CONDIMENT IN THE CLASSICS HALL OF FAME →

MAYONNAISE

Mayonnaise is the creamy condiment responsible for binding ingredients into a velvety mish-mash. It is also the perfect first layer of any great sandwich, before the piling on of personal and decisive ingredients within. Made from egg and oil, along with an acidic element to give it a bit more oomph, mayonnaise is a hit-or-miss condiment. After extensive research (probing people at the pub), I've come to realise that it is the most divisive condiment. It's either your all-time favourite, or you can't stand it. I fall into a minority category: I enjoy it, but don't need it for every meal.

Perhaps you're reading this and don't even like mayo. If so, **that is about to change**.

Though it originated in Spain as an invention of the French (see below for the details), most countries now make mayonnaise, and often in their own distinct way. First up, there's the classic, basic, mass-produced white mayonnaise that immediately springs to all our minds. This is gloopy and mild and is often used as a spread. It's made with the full egg, yolk and white, is the most universal and – if you hate mayonnaise – is probably the type you hate. Here is where you need to bear with me. There are so many other versions of mayonnaise that taste significantly different, as you will see when you feast your eyes (*almost* literally) on the map overleaf.

Everyone has their own mayonnaise of choice that they feel strongly about. Do you prefer a Japanese vinegary tang? Perhaps a French mustardy kick? Maybe even just a simple, creamy and versatile American mayo? My favourite type is made with just egg yolk and has a vinegar element to give the condiment a zing.

History of mayonnaise

Pretty weird word, huh? Ever wondered where it comes from?

In 1756, French forces under the command of Duc de Richelieu laid siege to Port Mahon in Minorca during the first European battle of the Seven Years' War. When the French won, the Duke's chef couldn't find any cream for his 'victory sauce'. As a French person, I can assure you this would have been a traumatic occurrence: we really love our creamy sauces. The chef had to scramble to serve the French officers what they wanted and were used to... so he invented a sauce with egg and oil and named it *mahonnaise* to celebrate the Port Mahon victory.

Mayonnaise around the world

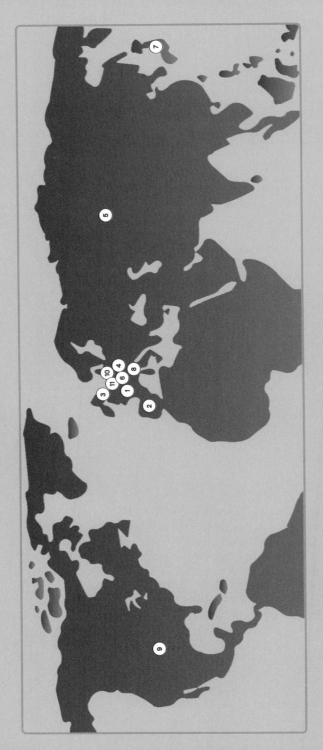

1 FRANCE

MADE FROM
Egg yolk and Dijon mustard (and vinegar or lemon juice)

ICONIC DISH
Egg mayonnaise

7 JAPAN

MADE FROM
Egg yolk and rice vinegar

ICONIC DISH
Okonomiyaki (vegetable pancake)

Regional flavour profiles subtly inform mayonnaise recipes. If you aren't paying attention, you might even miss the differences between them, but it's fascinating to look at how a mayonnaise can shift in response to cultural preferences. The condiment itself is a marker of culturally significant dishes, such as Russia's 'herring under a fur coat', the country's famous layered salad of cold cooked vegetables, eggs and fish. Mayonnaise is a big component of Russian salads, as in Soviet times it was a way to pack in more calories to bolster against Russia's harsh winters. Chile, in turn, has its iconic *completo* hotdogs. Chile loves mayo! Though it only became commercially available in the 1980s, now the country is in the top five consumers in the world annually. Meanwhile, Puerto Rico mixes mayonnaise and ketchup and eats this 'mayoketchup' with everything. Belgium takes the emulsion so seriously – after all, what else would they serve with their *moules frites*? – that, in 1955, the King signed a royal decree that mayonnaise had to contain a minimum 80 per cent fat and 7.5 per cent egg yolk.

2   SPAIN

MADE FROM
No egg! (just oil and garlic in their *alioli*)

ICONIC DISH
Patatas bravas

3   UK

MADE FROM
Whole egg and oil

ICONIC DISH
Coronation chicken

4   POLAND

MADE FROM
Egg yolk, lemon juice, mustard and vinegar

ICONIC DISH
Szalot salad

5   RUSSIA

MADE FROM
Whole egg, sugar, salt, vinegar, mustard, oil and dried milk

ICONIC DISH
Herring under a fur coat

6   GERMANY

MADE FROM
German mustard, sugar, egg yolk

ICONIC DISH
Kartoffelsalat

8   SWITZERLAND

MADE FROM
Egg yolk, vinegar, mustard

ICONIC DISH
Salad dressing

9   US

MADE FROM
Whole egg, sugar

ICONIC DISH
Sandwiches

10   THE NETHERLANDS

MADE FROM
Sugar, egg yolk, with a thinner texture

ICONIC DISH
Fritessaus ('fries sauce')

11   BELGIUM

MADE FROM
Egg yolk and oil, super-thick because of the deep-fried food (*frituur*) culture

ICONIC DISH
Moules frites (mussels, chips and mayo)

How to make mayonnaise

Making mayonnaise might seem intimidating, but, once you take that first leap of faith into tangy, creamy heaven, you'll learn to whip up a batch in no time and you won't look back. Like butter, mayonnaise is endlessly customisable. Due to its viscosity, it can be used not only as a spread, but also as a binder in your favourite protein-based salad (see overleaf for loads of options for those).

As with most of my recipes, this is easily adaptable to your palate and the contents of your fridge. All you really need is some oil, an egg, a form of acid (mustard, vinegar, lemon juice and so on) and salt. French mayonnaise includes egg yolk rather than whole egg, which gives a thicker, richer, scrumptious mouthfeel. The recipe below is a base in the truest sense: it was stolen from my French grandmother, Mamie Jeanne, and is now yours to impress with forever. It is my favourite mayonnaise because it tastes perfectly creamy, but hits you with a sharp acidic kick on the sides of your tongue. As always, feel free to switch it up to suit your taste; you'll be able to determine what your tastebuds respond to and how you can maximise your mayonnaise experience. Just remember: egg, oil, acid, salt.

This recipe can be hand beaten in a bowl, or you can cheat like I do and use a hand blender... but whip it all up in a tall vessel, to avoid splattering!

A bit of French folklore: *Si tu es enceinte tu ne peux pas monter une mayonnaise.* 'If you're pregnant, you can't whip up a mayo.' Go figure... but here's how to make it anyway.

WHAT YOU NEED

1 egg yolk
pinch of salt
1 hefty tbsp Dijon mustard,
   or to taste
60ml neutral oil (sunflower,
   safflower, rapeseed...)

40ml olive oil
2 tsp lemon juice
deep bowl and whisk,
   or hand blender and
   tall vessel

WHAT TO DO

1 Emulsify (whisk or blend) the egg yolk with the pinch of salt until yellow and fluffy. Make sure to use the deep bowl or tall vessel, so you don't splatter it all over your kitchen.

2 Add the mustard and continue to mix (you can always add more later, if you want more kick).

3 Combine the neutral and olive oils in a separate container.

4 Slowly drizzle the combined oils into the egg mixture, whisking or blending continuously. **Don't rush this**: the mixture will begin to thicken slowly, I promise! Trust the process.

5 Once all the oil is emulsified, add the lemon juice. (You can add vinegar if you prefer, but since there is vinegar in Dijon mustard, I prefer lemon juice here.)

6 There is no step 6, you've officially mastered making mayonnaise, so congratulations! Now feel free to play around with its flavours and add different oils, herbs, spices and so on. Homemade mayonnaise will keep, covered, in the fridge for about 1 week.

GREAT FLAVOURED MAYONNAISES

1 Roast garlic
   & thyme

2 Basil with
   sundried tomato

3 Preserved lemon
   & oregano

4 Truffle with
   roast shallot

5 Hot sauce & lime

6 Gochujang with
   spring onions

7 Parsley & lemon

PLAY AROUND WITH

8 Spices: allspice,
   cumin, ginger,
   nutmeg, paprika,
   pepper, sumac,
   turmeric

9 Herbs: basil,
   dill, oregano,
   sage, rosemary,
   parsley, thyme

FOR EACH 230G MAYONNAISE,
ADD AROUND 1 TBSP OF YOUR
FLAVOURING OF CHOICE

YOU CAN ALWAYS ADD MORE,
SO START SMALL

How to build a mayo-bound salad

Though its applications are innumerable, I find myself using mayonnaise primarily when making salads, in the American sense of that word. Any tuna, egg, chicken or potato salad (the list could go on and on) deserves a stunning mayonnaise to bind the ingredients together. And the trick to all salads is to play with texture, as that is key to maximum flavour pleasure.

MAYONNAISE

Flavoured (see page 37) or plain
+

PROTEIN

Chicken, chickpea, egg, tofu, tuna, potato (a bonus non-protein) and so on
+

CRUNCH

Celery, cucumber, fried onions or shallots, grapes, radishes, toasted nuts (toasted gives everything that extra oomph) such as almonds, hazelnuts, pine nuts or pistachios
+

FLAVOUR PUNCH

Candied jalapeño bites (see page 60), chilli flakes, dried cranberries, fennel seeds, furikake, ground pepper, herbs (basil, dill, oregano, rosemary), lemon zest, spring onions
+

SPLASH OF LIQUID

Apple cider vinegar (ACV), balsamic vinegar, Dijon mustard, hot sauce, ponzu (for homemade, see page 134), rice vinegar, soy sauce

PLAY WITH TEXTURE!

IF YOU'RE NOT INTO THIS TYPE OF SALAD

HERE ARE SOME OF MY MAYONNAISE-FRIENDLY SANDWICHES

Flavoured mayo sandwiches

Everyone loves a sandwich and, to my mind, mayonnaise is an essential element of a good bread filling. So here are five sarnies that showcase the various roles mayonnaise can play in your lunchtime.

Spicy tuna salad

+ chilli-pesto mayonnaise

Turkey pitta with grapes & celery

+ lemon-thyme mayonnaise

Basil, tomato & grilled veggie wrap

+ roast shallot mayonnaise

Coronation chicken with chopped apricots, currants & toasted almonds

+ curry-ginger mayonnaise

Egg salad on white bread

+ grainy mustard mayonnaise

MUSTARD

Due to its multiple flavour punches to the senses, mustard is my favourite condiment. Made from ground mustard seeds, vinegar and salt, it delivers a somewhat herbal taste as well as full-on acid and spice. My passion for mustard is immense. I should probably be embarrassed about my **love affair** with the yellow stuff, but the heart wants what it wants. I can't imagine eating a single meal without it: breakfast, lunch, dinner, snacks… It's fantastic with eggs, on a sandwich, as a thickening agent in a salad dressing, as a pre-roast or grill marinade, as a dip and, mainly, on a spoon. Mustard usage is, for me, immeasurable.

The idea of going to the cinema and having popcorn without mustard (use the mustard as a dip) is distressing. If civilisation was ending and I could only pick one ingredient from a shop, it would be mustard. No, of course I wouldn't be able to live off it, but I would be able to slather it on anything I found out in the wild.

Maybe it's the French in me? In the 8th century, Emperor Charlemagne hired monks to produce his own personal mustard. In the 14th century, Pope John XXII of Avignon created the position of Grand Moutardier du Pape, the Pope's chief mustard maker, to ensure there would always be someone nearby carrying his prized condiment. Finally, in the 21st century, Condiment Claire brought along a mini-Dijon mustard jar in her handbag wherever she went, **in case of emergencies**.

History of mustard

Mustard has been around since antiquity and was already popular in the courts of ancient Greece and Rome, where the condiment was used as medicine as well as to spice up dishes. The Romans eventually brought mustard to Northern France (where Dijon is located, in the Burgundy region) and it began to be cultivated by monks. In Dijon, the holy brothers took pride in perfecting their mustard, picking and grinding the seeds by hand before adding verjus (acidic unripe grape juice), in a process believed to have been invented in China more than 3,000 years ago. Much later, in the 1800s, the British began milling the inner part of the mustard seed into a fine powder. Since then, mustard powder has been used in cooking as well as in other mustards, such as American yellow mustard (no barbecue would be complete without it).

Don't make your own mustard!

I won't often tell you not to make something yourself, but mustard is a notable exception. It usually turns out too grainy, or just not quite right. Shop-bought mustard is great. If you make your own mustard anyway, or want to try it, that is perfectly fine! It's actually more than fine – **I'm impressed** – but it's just not for me.

An illustrated guide to mustards and their perfect pairings

AMERICAN VS HONEY VS
BROWN VS GERMAN
VS GRAINY VS
DIJON VS HOT

MY DEFINITIVE MUSTARD GUIDE

AMERICAN YELLOW MUSTARD	**HONEY MUSTARD**	**AMERICAN SPICY BROWN MUSTARD**	**GERMAN MUSTARD**
Barbecue's MVP (most valuable player)	The gateway mustard for those who think they don't like mustard	A coarse-textured condiment	(Not the same as American spicy brown, but looks similar!)
MADE FROM	**MADE FROM**	**MADE FROM**	**MADE FROM**
Yellow mustard seeds (mild), vinegar, water and turmeric for colour	Yellow mustard seeds and honey	Ground brown mustard seeds (hot) and spices	Many variations, depending on region, but most common is a blend of both yellow and brown seeds
PAIRING IDEAS	**PAIRING IDEAS**	**PAIRING IDEAS**	**PAIRING IDEAS**
Barbecue, sauces, hotdogs, burgers and pretzels. There is something about the turmeric in it that marries so well with anything warming, such as roast sweet potatoes, pumpkin, curried chicken or coconut-based broths	Poultry, pork, dipping and crudités, as a foil to spicy food, with roast root vegetables	A classic in NYC deli sandwiches, especially with salty dark meats such as pastrami, or to give a kick to milder white meats such as chicken apple sausage	Fatty meat (think Oktoberfest), so sausages, pretzels, charcuterie boards, or dark green herby dishes with spiky greens and herbs such as kale, curly parsley or tarragon

Mustard is very territory-based. Each variety has a particular flavour which pairs specifically with the foods on that culture's table. If you understand these pairings, you will open yourself up to exciting worlds of distinct international flavour.

Sunday roast without hot English mustard? Charcuterie board or *steak frites* without Dijon? Backyard barbecue without American yellow mustard? Oktoberfest without sausage and German mustard? *Gyeoja-naengchae* (cold noodle salad) without Korean mustard? Here is your basic guide on how to use every mustard for a specific occasion, to fully maximise condiment-induced pleasure.

Basics

Yellow (also called white) mustard seeds	⟶	Mild
Brown mustard seeds	⟶	Hot
Black mustard seeds	⟶	**Very** hot

Vinegar delays spicy-heat transfer to the taste receptors, while water does not. So mustard that contains more water (such as English mustard) will be more immediately pungent. Some types of mustards, such as Dijon, also use wine, verjus, beer or lemon juice: the more acidic the liquid, the less heat a mustard will give off.

GRAINY MUSTARD	DIJON	HOT MUSTARD !!
Texture texture texture!	A silky spoonful that packs a kick	(English mustard, Chinese mustard, Korean mustard...)
MADE FROM	**MADE FROM**	**MADE FROM**
Brown seeds (hot) that haven't been ground down – so they're like mustard caviar! – plus wine	Brown seeds, white verjus (unripe grape juice) or vinegar and white wine	Powdered mustard seeds with water, no vinegar. English mustard uses a brown and yellow mustard seed mix, while Korean and Chinese mustards use only brown seeds. The flavour resembles horseradish
PAIRING IDEAS	**PAIRING IDEAS**	**PAIRING IDEAS**
Charcuterie, cheese, ham, mashed potatoes, adding to a quiche or a cheese soufflé, in a ham sandwich, with oily canned fish or smooth egg mayonnaise	Anything French: vinaigrette, sauces, mayo or steak. Since it has a massive flavour punch, I love to add it to blander foods such as eggs and popcorn. Its silky-smooth texture also lends itself to being a great sauce thickener, marinade base, or the perfect injection of acidity to dips and jams, such as hummus or chilli jam	English mustard is used with sausages and roast beef, or roast pork with crackling; Chinese mustard is also used with pork, or with fried food; Korean mustard is used in a sauce for cold noodles

A day in mustard

As always, there are no wrong combinations in the world of condiments, so here are some fun ways I like to celebrate mustard.

Everyone asks me how I can possibly go through so much mustard, but when it's present at every meal, it's easily done. With just a single dollop, you can add acidity, spice, salt or even sweetness to a dish, depending on your choice. While mustard allows you to alter the level of punch in anything you eat, it can also change the overall texture: the smoothness of Dijon, the crackle of a grainy version, the thick velvety texture of honey mustard. All these will inform your experience of every bite. You are choosing the flavour that will linger in your mouth: will you go for spicy? Sweet? Herbal?

My rules of thumb

- I prefer to cook with Dijon mustard, due to its smooth texture and the punch it gives. Feel free to make a more supply-based decision, cooking with whatever mustard is in your kitchen.

- A side dish should be an exciting addition to your main course, not just bland vegetables you feel you ought to eat, so I always use a distinct mustard for sides, either flavoured or with texture.

- Don't forget about Japanese pickled mustard leaves. These always give a nice crunch to a rice bowl.

I admit, I have mixed mustard with every condiment. I have stirred it into butter, chilli jam, chutney, guacamole, honey, hot sauce, hummus, jam, maple syrup, miso, tzatziki... the list goes on. The best part? For me, the combination of flavours works nearly every single time, which perhaps proves that flavour is so deeply rooted in nostalgia and positive childhood experiences.

BREAKFAST

1 Dijon on avocado toast

2 Grainy Dijon scrambled eggs

3 Ham, cheese & grainy mustard quiche

LUNCH & SNACKS

1 *Vinaigrette à la moutarde* on your salad of choice

2 Reuben sandwich with spicy brown mustard

3 Fish, egg, potato or chicken salad bound with mustard in the mix (see page 38)

4 Dijon & hummus mish-mash

5 Popcorn dipped in Dijon or American yellow mustard

6 Grapes & grainy mustard

7 Tortilla chips & honey mustard

DINNER & SIDES

1 Lemon-tarragon-Dijon white fish

2 American yellow mustard-coated fried burgers

3 Miso-honey mustard roast chicken

4 Pork chops, English mustard & apple sauce

5 Grainy mustard haricots verts

6 Leeks vinaigrette

7 Grainy Dijon mashed potatoes, or celeriac

8 Honey mustard carrots & parsnips

BUTTER

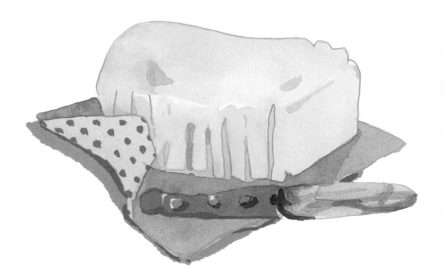

Including butter in my Classics chapter is perhaps a little bold, because many of you might argue that butter is not a condiment. (It is.)

There are two different categories of butter: ingredient butter and condiment butter. The butter you use for cooking – ingredient butter – (the type you might use to make an omelette) is **not** a condiment. It is 'whatever' butter. It's the cheapest kind you can buy, that you pop in your fridge or freezer for future use. It's great for cooking and baking, but won't excite you in a sandwich, melting over pancakes or squashed between two halves of a radish. But the butter you use as a spread or a dip in that way **is** a condiment. In my opinion, it is butter you should either make yourself or prepare to invest in. It's the kind of butter you could, and should, eat by the chunkful. A delectable fatty slab of yellow solidified cream with big crystals of salt is my personal favourite.

There are also two types of butter consumers: soft butter aficionados and hard butter lovers. Personally, I like to see toothmarks in my condiment butter, so I am an adamant hard butter fan. For the utmost satisfaction when eating butter, I like to feel it in my teeth, the smoosh in between my molars with the occasional surprise salty crunch from sel gris. There is truly nothing like it. Some prefer soft butter, the kind you can slather on lusciously with no effort: I don't judge them, but it's just not for me.

In my kitchen, I keep my ingredient butter on the counter for cooking and baking, but my condiment butters (yes, plural) have their own dedicated shelf in the fridge.

History of butter ← ANCIENT BOTOX FIT FOR THE GODS

You may be thinking: who in the world first decided to milk an animal, make cream, shake it up endlessly until weird little yellow clumps formed and then squeeze those together and **EAT** them? The story goes that, in about 8,000 BCE, an African herder found that a sheepskin container of milk strapped to the back of one of his sheep had curdled into butter after being tossed around on their walk. And though there is also evidence of butter written on a limestone tablet from 2,000 BCE, there is more evidence of the scrumptious fatty condiment and its fun history if we flash-forward a bit.

As it turns out, the ancient world did not actually eat butter for yummy purposes, but rather thought of it as a practical tool. While ancient Romans swallowed butter for coughs, or rubbed it on physical injuries, ancient Egyptians used a mix of butter, dirt and sawdust in the mummification process to plump up human skin. Ancient Botox, as it were.

Butter has also been a major player in religion. Ever heard of ghee? A type of clarified butter (though the cooking technique is slightly different), Hindus have been offering Lord Krishna, one of their deities, containers of solidified yellow ghee for more than 3,000 years. It is considered the sacred fat and a marker of creation.

The Bible also mentions butter as a food for celebration: Abraham and Sarah offer the three angels butter, meat and milk. Up until the 1600s, butter-eating was even widely banned for Christians during Lent. This was particularly difficult for Northern Europeans, because they did not have access to cooking oil. The rich always seem to get around these issues though. Wealthy butter fanatics could pay the church a hefty sum to be allowed to eat it; in fact, in Rouen in Northern France, an entire tower – La Tour de Beurre – was financed and built in the Cathedral using these butter tithes.

Salted butter was not, though, considered a food fit for the gods; in fact, it was looked down upon. Salt is a preserving agent that keeps butter fresh for longer. The higher class did not need this – they could afford to buy sweet butter whenever they wanted it – and so they had the luxury of serving unsalted butter that would turn rancid quickly. **(How boring and tasteless is snobbery.)**

Overseas, the first ever student revolt in America was provoked by butter. Perhaps I feel strongly about this because it happened at my alma mater, but it is pretty iconic if you ask me. In 1766, students at Harvard were served spoiled butter in the dining hall (and now I want to know if it was posh unsalted butter). The students were already upset by the quality of food served and the rancid butter was the last straw. They revolted for days.

Cooking fats around the world

When used in cooking, fat concentrates flavour by bringing everything together and creating a cohesive entity: it is the ultimate flavour carrier.

Fat use is heavily dependent upon geography. Mountainous or verdant regions suited to animal husbandry – think the Alps, or Ireland – tend to use animal fat in the form of butter or lard. On the other hand, more arid, warmer regions, such as Southern Italy or Greece, use olive oil as the primary fat, in both cooking and as a condiment. Countries with varied climates often use a combination. France, for instance, produces butter in the North, neutral oils and butter in the centre and olive oil in the South.

Around the world, the types of fat commonly used in food immensely influence a country's cooking. They are a major symbol of culinary identity, determining how and what is put on the table, the flavour profile of its inhabitants, ideal food and drink pairings and more.

Obviously, this is not an exhaustive list; it is a broad indication of who cooks where with what.

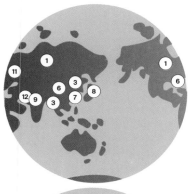

1   BUTTER

Northern Europe, Scandinavia and Russia, North America and Canada, Northern Italy, Morocco and India

2   GOOSE AND DUCK FAT

South West France

3   PORK FAT

Latin America, Eastern Europe, Emilia Romagna, Spain, China and Thailand

4   SUET

England and Ireland

5   OLIVE OIL

Mediterranean, Middle East, North Africa

6   PEANUT OIL

Southern USA, China, Southern Africa

7   SESAME OIL

China, Korea, Japan and South East Asia

8   RICE BRAN OIL

Japan

9   MUSTARD OIL

India, Pakistan, Bangladesh, Nepal and Kashmir

10 GHEE

India, Bangladesh, Pakistan, Egypt

11 SCHMALTZ (CHICKEN FAT)

Eastern Europe

12 COCONUT OIL

Caribbean, Pakistan, Bangladesh, India

13 RED PALM FRUIT OIL (DENDE OIL)

West Africa, Brazil

How to make butter

Butter is hands-down my favourite condiment to play around with. First, it's the easiest to make, as all you need is cream. The method of transforming it into a solid is up to you: **elbow grease or an electric mixer?** Using an electric mixer will obviously be much faster, but I find churning by hand far more satisfying. Making butter is fun and I find it makes a much-appreciated gift, especially when paired with a loaf of crusty bread, either homemade or shop-bought.

How long it takes to make it, though, depends on fat percentage and temperature, as well as the mode of churning. For instance, in the UK, where the fat content of cream can be as high as nearly 50 per cent, it will be quicker. In the USA, where the fat content is closer to 35 per cent, it will take longer.

The ideal whipping temperature is around 18°C. If cream is too cold it will take a long time to whip; too hot and it will be gloopy. Don't artificially heat the cream, just leave it out on the counter until it reaches temperature.

I love my butter salted, but if you're an unsalted aficionado, you do you. The sweet butter solids are a deliciously creamy canvas upon which to play with a multitude of flavours and textures (see opposite). Make it salty, sweet or spicy; it's your choice.

WHAT YOU NEED
container of double cream (usually sold around 300ml), **the higher the fat content, the better, at room temperature** (see above)
electric mixer (or see above)
large bowl
ice cubes

WHAT TO DO

1 Whip the cream. It will begin to thicken and then form what you will recognise as whipped cream. Keep going.

2 It will get thicker and almost seem pasty. Keep going. When you want to give up, keep going.

3 The cream is about to 'break': pea-sized pieces will form and it will look wet. Now be careful, or you will get splashed! The cream will begin to solidify into dense yellow chunks and separate from a cloudy liquid. This liquid is buttermilk: keep it in the fridge to give pancakes, biscuits, fried chicken and waffles a fluffy texture and tangy kick.

4 Fill the bowl with cold water and add the ice.

5 Once the butter appears fully formed, quickly squeeze it into a lump, but don't handle it too much or the heat from your hands will melt it.

6 Place the lump of butter into the bowl of iced water. Squeeze and rinse the butter to remove the excess buttermilk.

7 On a clean surface, or in a chilled bowl, spread out and mix the butter with your ingredients of choice: salt, chilli flakes, herbs or spices.

8 Now load the butter into a ramekin, or roll it in baking parchment to form a log. Homemade butter will last in the fridge for a few weeks, if not more, and it also freezes nicely. You'll know if it has gone bad, as it will stop smelling like butter and start smelling of cheese.

GREAT FLAVOURED BUTTERS

1	2	3
4	5	6
8	9	10
11	12	13
14	17	18

1 Maple syrup
2 Fig with cardamom
3 Cinnamon & vanilla
4 Honeyed rosemary
5 Miso with brown sugar
6 Caraway
7 Roast garlic (or shallot)
8 Herbes de Provence
9 Parsley
10 Sage
11 Chive
12 Chilli and basil
13 Lemon zest with harissa
14 Salt & pepper
15 Olive
16 Miso with seaweed
17 Anchovy
18 Truffle

PLAY ABOUT WITH THE QUANTITIES OF FLAVOURINGS UNTIL YOU FIND A BALANCE YOU LIKE

Roast chicken & vegetables

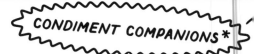
CONDIMENT COMPANIONS *

Full disclosure: I used to **HATE** chicken. And not just dislike it, but actively truly hate it, because I found it so bland and dry. The only place in the world I would eat it was in the French countryside, at my adopted grandmother's farm *(probably because she would twist its neck and murder the poor thing hours before dinner time)*. Tastebuds change with time and I learned to love a good roast chicken, perhaps because of the ease of this one one-dish recipe, as well as – of course – the condiment opportunities that can be seized alongside it.

This is the easiest, juiciest roast chicken: just pop it all into the oven at the same time. If some vegetables get darker than others, so be it, I don't mind a little char or crunch. Though I usually just toss in whatever veg I have, my all-time favourite combo is a *very* lemon-and-shallot-heavy roast chicken snuggled among carrots, parsnips, small potatoes, cauliflower, Pink Lady apples and Brussels sprouts.

My only request is that you invest in a good chicken; make sure it had a good life, you'll taste it. I limit meat intake and want my consumption to make a positive impact, so try to support farmers with good practices who care about their animals.

WHAT YOU NEED

1.5kg chicken
herbs of choice
   bunch of thyme, rosemary
   or herbes de Provence
2 lemons
olive oil
salt
root veg, in season,
   of choice
   beetroots, carrots,
   celeriac, fennel, parsnips,
   potatoes, radishes, sweet
   potatoes, swedes, turnips

3 onions
3 shallots
other vegetable ideas
   asparagus, Brussels sprouts, cauliflower,
   cherry tomatoes, courgettes, green beans,
   peppers, pumpkin, squash
fun additions (optional)
   apples and pears (these give the entire
   roast a nice overall sweetness and pair
   wonderfully with Dijon mustard)
pepper
large roasting tin or baking tray
   (preferably deep)

WHAT TO DO

1. Take the chicken out of the fridge 1 hour before roasting.

2. Preheat the oven to 200°C.

3. Place the chicken in the tin or tray and stuff your herbs of choice and slices from 1 whole lemon into its cavity. Rub olive oil all over the outside, then salt the bird well and scatter with more herbs.

4. Prepare your vegetables and fun additions, if using: chop them up and place in the tin or tray. *Add as much variety as you'd like, but smaller pieces roast (and char) faster, so try to keep them all the same size.*

5. Drizzle your veg with oil, salt, pepper and the juice of the remaining lemon. Toss in the lemon shell too, then roast for 20–25 minutes.

6. Reduce the oven temperature to 180°C for another 45–60 minutes, depending on the strength of your oven, or until the juices run clear when the bird is pierced between its leg and thigh.

* Though the ways in which to use condiments are almost limitless – salads, sandwiches, crudités, desserts – I have included in this book a handful of **Condiment Companions** for you: non-condiment recipes with which to eat condiments! Brief and simple, these will never let you down. Each is the perfect vehicle for your current condiment obsession *(when just eating it on a spoon starts to get a bit boring)*.

↳ *FOR CHICKEN*

FAVOURITE CONDIMENTS
1 Dijon mustard and flavoured Dijon. I will have at least four on the table ready for a chicken and vegetable mish-mash.
2 Rosé jelly (see page 100): rosé wine and poultry work well together, so why drink it if you can eat it?
3 Herb jelly (see page 99). This makes sense because of the herbs you have already roasted with the chicken. It brings up the herby and citrusy notes and it is also lovely with Dijon mustard.
4 Orange-coloured jams and chutneys (see page 88): apricot and peach bring brightness to the comforting flavours of a roast. They're especially nice on white veggies such as cauliflower and potatoes. Don't ask me why, just give it a try! Find out what colour combos work for you.
5 Purple-coloured jams or chutneys (see page 88): plum, grape, blackcurrant and blueberry all pair surprisingly well when mixed with Dijon mustard. Their deep, cosy taste is perfect for a roast chicken evening.

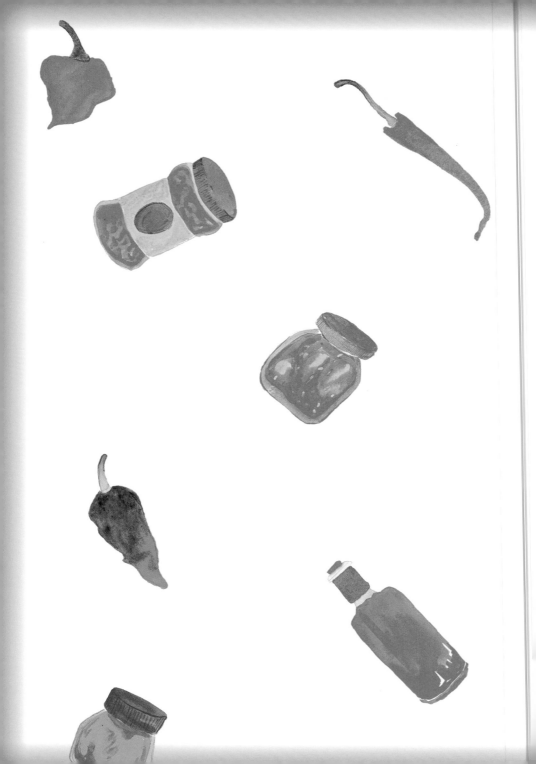

SPICY

HOT SAUCE + CHILLIES:
FROM TORTURE DEVICES
TO PLEASURE ENHANCERS ↘

Hot sauces, chilli pastes and jams: these are the condiments you can't live without, while having no idea why you love them quite so much. They cause you pain, sweats and ringing ears… and you can't get enough.

Chilli-heat is not a taste. Rather, when you eat something spicy, you feel its flavour (yes flavour, not taste) due to nerves that trigger heat and pain receptors. These overwhelming physical feelings are due to the endorphin and dopamine release caused by capsaicin, the component of a chilli that sets off the feeling of heat in the body. Though it's a common belief that the heat is contained in a chilli's seed, the capsaicin is actually located in those white membranes surrounding it. Yes, if you bite on a seed, it will most likely be hot, but that's only because it's been attached to the white spongey lining.

Spicy condiments come in all shapes and sizes: fresh, dried, powdered, liquids, pastes, sweet sticky sauces and more. And every culture has its favourite source of heat, as well as a distinct cuisine to pair with it. Whole books have been written about these, but I will limit this chapter to a core selection that can open up the spicier side of your palate (and see page 181 for further reading, if you want even more heat).

Heat-inducing condiments are some of my favourites to play around with, and yet I could not tolerate them until my early twenties. Blame my paternal blood: the French have traditionally never used much chilli, so their lack of experience tends to scare them away from it. One of my best friends is Chinese and, when we moved in together in New York after college, I just knew I had to get over my low capsaicin tolerance. Let's just say she trained me well, with fantastic flavours in our kitchen as well as long evenings experimenting with bike deliveries of blisteringly hot Thai green papaya salads. It did the trick and my tastebuds feel stronger for it: I am proud to say that I love chilli now.

I grew up in LA, with Mexican fruit stallholders on most street corners dumping chilli, lime juice and salt on your fruit of choice. This was one of my favourite snacks growing up, as the heat really is quite mild, alongside the mouth-puckering bright acidity of lime, a full sweetness from ripe fruit and that surprising touch of salt to round it all off. I enjoyed the blend of flavours because it felt warm (not hot) and gave off a lingering, almost calming sensation. Now, I always have Mexican tajin spice handy in my kitchen. I started trying new hot sauces with fruit, specifically mango (frozen mango chunks with Cholula hot sauce is one of my favourite snacks). Margarita fan? Make it spicy. After the first drink, your tastebuds become semi-numb anyway.

But my conscious self-training to **embrace the heat** was never about wanting to be able to eat spicy food. It was about a yen to appreciate diverse chillies for their different flavour notes, as well as to be able to travel to faraway places without having to ask for a more Westernised, less-hot version of a traditional dish.

Measuring heat: the Scoville scale

In 1912, while attempting to create a heat-inducing ointment, pharmacist Wilbur Scoville invented a method to measure and categorise the heat levels of different chillies. If you're a hot sauce fan, you probably know your favourite chilli's Scoville Heat Unit (SHU). To those of us who don't live off hot sauce, the Scoville scale is the measurement of the number of times capsaicin *(yes you know this word now, the spicy component of chillies)* needs to be diluted by a sugar solution until you can no longer detect heat. (When sugar is added to water, it becomes a neutralising element to the heat created by capsaicin.) A regular sweet red pepper – the sort you'd slice and use as a crudité – has 0 SHU, whereas the notorious Carolina Reaper chilli has more than 1,400,000 SHU. ↖ *OUCH*

Even if you don't consider yourself a fan of heat, you most likely have some capsaicin hiding somewhere in your kitchen (see overleaf).

ALL OF THESE ARE DOUBLE-WHAMMY HEAT-CALMING CONDIMENT COMBOS

Taming the burn

Heat also allows for **fun flavour combinations**. When you are playing with spicy condiments, try to think of heat-mellowing partners for them. What are the neutralising agents that go further than simply quelling heat and actually entice you to eat more? Sugar and dairy are always good bets. Perhaps a Tomato-vanilla-basil jam? What about a Bright ranch dressing? Some Tzatziki? (See pages 87, 144 and 162.)

Scoville pepper chart

PADRÓN PEPPER

50-2,500
(Some are spicier than others,
each produces a different
amount of capsaicin)

CHIPOTLE CHILLI

5,000-8,000

PIMENT D'ESPELETTE

500-4,000
(mild French chilli flakes)

ARBOL CHILLI

15,000-30,000

PEPPERONCINI

100-500
(mild Italian chilli flakes)

POBLANO CHILLI

1,000-1,500

CAYENNE PEPPER

30,000-50,000

STANDARD HOT HONEY

500

JALAPEÑO CHILLI

2,500-10,000

TABASCO SAUCE

30,000-50,000

RED PEPPER

0

STANDARD CHILLI JAM

300-3,000
Depending on
the brand

SERRANO CHILLI

10,000-23,000

1,000   5,000   20,000

0
SHU

BLACK PEPPER

The sensation of about 30,000 SHU, though pepper
does not contain capsaicin; the hot feeling it gives
comes from a chemical compound called piperine

**THAI BIRD
EYE CHILLI**

50,000-100,000

HABANERO PEPPER

100,000-350,000

**CAROLINA REAPER
CHILLI**

1,400,000-2,200,000

**SCOTCH BONNET
CHILLI**

100,000-350,000

**TRINIDAD
SCORPION
CHILLI**

1,200,000- 2,000,000

**HOT
CHEETOS**

50,000

**PURE
CAPSAICIN**

15,000,000-16,000,000

**GHOST
PEPPER**

855,000-1,050,000

50,000	100,000	500,000	1,000,000	2,000,000

16,000,000
SHU

Candied jalapeño bites

I'm taking a moment here to introduce you to a superhero recipe of mine. These are a staple in my fridge. They're my favourite *(and most requested)* gift for friends and family. They're perfect for people who like heat, or for those who like sweet, sour, salty... you get the point: everyone **LOVES** them. It's hard not to put them on everything. They're a great chewy pop of sweetness, heat and tang all at once.

This recipe is a double-whammy gift to your fridge: not only do you get delectable, sweet jalapeños with an acidic bite, but you're also left with a sumptuous spicy syrup to use in cocktails, salad dressings or to reuse to hot-candy yet another ingredient!

Contrary to their complex taste, this recipe is quite basic. The liquid – let's call it the 'candying brine' – is magical. Though this recipe is for jalapeños, I've used the brine for everything from red chillies and grapes to rhubarb.

You can thank me later.

WHAT YOU NEED
10–15 jalapeños, depending on their size
240ml apple cider vinegar (ACV)
400g sugar
1 tsp ground ginger
saucepan
sterilised jar (see page 74)

WHAT TO DO

1 Slice the jalapeños into thick circles.

2 Put the vinegar in the saucepan with the sugar and ground ginger and bring to the boil, stirring to make sure the sugar has fully dissolved.

3 Add the jalapeño rings and simmer until they turn from bright green to a darker forest green. This can take 5–10 minutes depending on their size. Once you've achieved this colour, turn off the heat and put both jalapeños and their delicious spicy syrup into the sterilised jar.

4 Pop them in the fridge, give to your friends, eat immediately, it's really up to you. They keep for months in the fridge.

PAIRING IDEAS

1. With breakfast toasts *(avocado, scrambled eggs, bagel & cream cheese, cottage cheese, ricotta)*

2. On sourdough or baguette with butter & strawberry jam

3. In devilled eggs

4. With caprese salad

5. Or Greek salad

6. With soft white cheeses *(mozzarella, burrata, Brie, Camembert)*

7. In wraps or sandwiches *(grilled veggies, chicken, tuna, turkey)*

8. In barbecue dishes *(hotdogs, burgers, grilled sweetcorn)*

9. In potato salad

10. With tacos

11. With grapes

12. Or watermelon

13. In cocktails

I HAD REAL TROUBLE LIMITING THIS LIST

OK, I'VE INTRODUCED YOU TO CANDIED JALAPEÑO FANDOM, NOW ON TO SOME HOT SAUCE LOVE

HOT SAUCE

History of hot sauce

The first ever recorded condiment was chilli paste, back in 7,000 BCE in Mesoamerica. (Yes, butter is estimated to have been made before that, see page 47, but we don't have concrete evidence.) Since chilli-based condiments have been around for thousands of years, their histories are complex, their uses diverse and their impact on society enormous. Used as a means of torture, medicine, currency and flavour, the chilli plant has radiated heat throughout most of human history, and in so many distinct geographical regions that it has made itself indispensable to almost every food culture. This is despite the fact that it isn't necessary to the human body for either calories or nutrients, it's simply enjoyed for its flavour and burn. **The chilli isn't about survival, it's about our love for it.**

As the oldest condiment, chilli paste shows us just how important the sharing of ingredients and ideas around the globe has always been. We've been able to exchange chilli-knowledge with different cultures, peoples and lands. Today, the happy results of this are clear in the most beautiful amalgamation of flavours, recipes and uses for chilli in all its forms: cooked, dried, powdered, pickled and raw (*particularly tasty in spicy margaritas*).

The first hot sauce was most likely a simple paste of mashed chillies and water. Nothing elaborate, just a purely delicious mix. This paste, however, was not solely consumed as a condiment. It was also used as both medicine and torture device.

Aztecs used their native chillies to exert power and dominance over others. Burning them to create a **capsaicin smokescreen** was among their most powerful weapons. The spicy fire – **just like pepper spray** – could completely debilitate the enemy by blinding and suffocating them. Ironically, Aztec soldiers commonly had chillies in their pockets to use for food when they weren't deploying them as part of their personal arsenal. Yes, chillies were used as weapons of war, but they were also employed at home, both as food and punishment... Children who had misbehaved were commonly placed above smoking chillies, or forced to eat them raw.

AZTEC CHILLI TORTURE

63

Chillies around the world

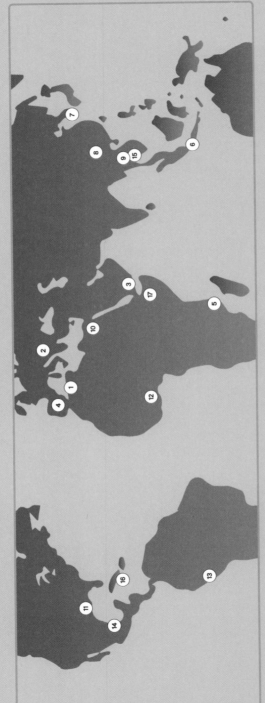

In every region and culture, a signature heat-delivery condiment has been developed. The Portuguese brought chillies to their African colonies at the end of the 15th century and they took immediate root there, since the plants do so well in hotter climates. Eating chillies suited the inhabitants of the warmer countries as well: perspiration cools the body and we all know how strong chilli can affect your sweat glands.

5 PERI PERI SAUCE

Meaning 'pepper pepper', this originated in Mozambique and is made from bird eye chilli, lemon juice, bay leaf and vinegar

6 SAMBAL

This ubiquitous Indonesian condiment has chillies ground with ginger, sugar, shallots, vinegar and sometimes shrimp paste

12 SHITO

This Ghanaian smoky concoction combines dried fish with ginger, garlic, spices and chillies

13 AJI

Another word for 'chilli' in South America, *aji* can also refer to a spicy sauce made with herbs, alliums and sometimes tomatoes. It is very popular in Peru and has many variants, such as the bright orange *aji amarillo* and *aji panca*

1 HARISSA

This originated in Tunisia, spread throughout North Africa and remains a staple. Unsurprisingly, since the area was and still is a hub of the spice trade, harissa is a blend of chilli paste *(made from both red and Baklouti chillies)*, oil and various spices such as cumin and coriander. The word itself derives from *harasa*, the Arabic verb for 'to crush or pound'

2 HUNGARIAN PAPRIKA

When Ottoman Turks invaded Hungary in 1526, they brought the paprika chilli with them. Though it was initially used as ornamental foliage for noblemens' castles, the spice was eventually recorded in an 18th-century cookbook. Hungarian paprika is made by drying the pepper and pulverising it into a powder. It's mild and sweet and has become a crucial part of Hungarian cuisine, such as in their famous goulash

3 ZHUG

This popular bright green and chunky hot sauce originated in Yemen and has made it as far afield as Israel. It is composed of distinct herbs, toasted spices and peppers

4 PIMENTÓN (SPANISH PAPRIKA)

Unlike Hungarian paprika, pimentón has a deep and smoky flavour. This chilli was brought directly to Spain from the Americas by Columbus in the 16th century. Back then, in Spain, it was only used by the monks of the Yuste Monastery, but eventually spread across the country and has become a decisive element in many of the nation's dishes

7 GOCHUJANG

Korea's staple chilli paste. Before the Portuguese introduced chillies to East Asia in the 16th century, the equivalent was known as 후추장, or 'pepper paste', as it was made with – shocker – black pepper. Once chillies arrived, Koreans replaced black pepper with *gochugaru* – a red chilli powder – and mashed it with glutinous rice powder, fermented soy beans and salt

8 CHILLI OIL

Oil infused with chillies is used everywhere in East Asian – especially Sichuan – cooking

9 NAM PRIK

A Thai condiment whose name means 'chilli water'

10 SHATTA

From Egypt, this is a thick paste of chillies, olive oil and tomato

11 TABASCO

Tabasco is one of the many business-savvy condiment empires. In the 1860s, during the American Civil War, ex-banker Edmund McIlhenny lost his fortune and moved to the salt-rich Avery Island in Louisiana. He planted Tabasco peppers and began making hot sauce. His tactic of solely supplying prominent establishments – restaurants and gentlemen's clubs – left an impression on many people at once, without individuals having to buy the sauce to give it a shot. Once the flavour became familiar, people wanted the sauce at their house and McIlhenny began selling it to grocery stores

14 CHOLULA

Named after the oldest still-inhabited city in the North American continent, Cholula is made from a family recipe which blends native Arbol and Pequin chillies with regional spices. The woman pictured on the famous bottles, Camila Harrison, was the matriarch of the Cholula company family

15 SRIRACHA

Invented in 1949 in the town of Si Racha in South East Thailand by Ms Thanom Chakkapak. In 1975, David Tran, a Vietnamese sauce-maker and refugee, fled to California. He named his sauce in homage to the area in which the recipe originated

16 SCOTCH BONNET HOT SAUCES

A very hot yet sweet chilli found both in the Caribbean and in West Africa. Scotch bonnet's unique fruity, tropical flavour is a key marker in jerk marinade and lends itself to traditional Caribbean dishes such as rice and peas. It is also used to make a popular Haitian hot sauce called *ti malice*, or 'lil mischief' in French Creole *(named after the punch it packs)*

17 AWAZE

Warming spices and chillies are mixed into this Ethiopian blend, traditionally made with honey wine

TIME TO GET INTO SOME FUN RECIPES. PLEASE DO NOT USE THESE AS TORTURE DEVICES. THANK YOU VERY MUCH

How to make hot sauce

When it comes to hot sauce, I like to take my time. I find that fermented hot sauce gives off more tang and depth of flavour, but the first step – fermenting chillies – can take from five days to two weeks, depending on location: it is slower in London than in Southern California! Committing to fermenting is like having a goldfish: take care of it and it will bring you joy, but it won't need all your time.

The good news is that there are **SO** many great hot sauces on the market. I am not going to pretend that I **only** use my homemade hot sauce, because that would be a big fat lie. As long as your tastebuds are happy, you should be too.

However, if you choose to make it, hot sauce is a great condiment to play with. Make it mild, devilishly spicy, red, green, herby, citrusy, fruity...

Pro tip: Stick to similar-coloured ingredients. **Either** red and orange chillies (Thai bird eye, habanero) + spices **or** green chillies (jalapeño, serrano) + herbs. Not only do these flavour profiles match up well, but the strategy will also prevent you ending up with an unappetisingly light-brownish sauce.

Now you *could* make this without fermentation and simply roast the ingredients, then blend them once cooled, but I think the flavour isn't as special.

WHAT YOU NEED

4 chillies
½ onion
1 garlic clove
sea salt
filtered water
plastic gloves
glass jar
fermenting weights
sterilised bottles (see page 74)

WHAT TO DO

Ferment

1   Put on your gloves and please don't touch your eyes. Clean your chillies and slice to remove the seeds.

2   Combine and weigh your prepared chillies, ½ onion and garlic clove, make a note of their combined weight, then place in the jar.

3   Measure out 2.5 per cent of the weight in salt. Add it to the jar.

4   Fill the jar 80 per cent of the way up with filtered water, close and shake until the salt has dissolved.

5   Open up the jar again and place fermenting weights on top to fully submerge your ingredients in their salt brine.

6   Close the lid, store the jar in a cool dark place and burp* daily until you find it has fermented to your liking *(there will be loads of little bubbles)*. Depending on the climate, it should take around 1 week.

* Burping a jar just means opening it slightly and letting out the air pressure caused by the fermentation. The little popping sound is extremely satisfying, so prepare to love burping from now on!

Blend

7 Once you're satisfied with your fermented chillies, strain the ingredients and reserve their brine.

8 Blend your ingredients (alongside any herb or spice your heart desires) and add as much of the fermenting brine as you'd like; some people like thicker hot sauce, while others prefer it very liquid.

9 Strain yet again to make sure there are no chunkies.

10 Bottle up! This keeps for a few months in the fridge.

HOT SAUCE: THE GOLDEN RULES

My recipe

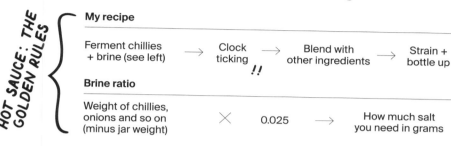

Ferment chillies + brine (see left) → Clock ticking !! → Blend with other ingredients → Strain + bottle up

Brine ratio

Weight of chillies, onions and so on (minus jar weight) × 0.025 → How much salt you need in grams

Feel free to deviate from the base recipe here and add your own spicy flair. You can change the level of heat with different chillies, add sweetness with fruit, acidity with vinegar and more. It's the perfect blank canvas, so make it your own. Over the next few pages are four variations that are my favourite go-tos when I want to get funky.

All four recipes follow the same principle as the base recipe. Ferment your chillies, onion and garlic (and any other ingredients you'd like to ferment), strain, blend, strain again and – *voilà* – you've got yourself the personalised hot sauce of dreams. Great for gifting, great for yourself.

BE WARY WHEN PICKING YOUR CHILLIES! SOME PACK A BIGGER PUNCH THAN OTHERS

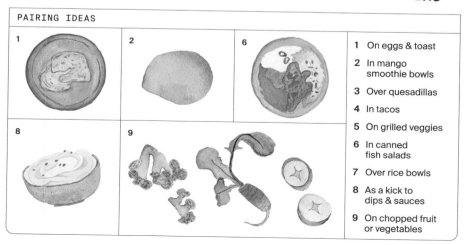

PAIRING IDEAS

1 On eggs & toast
2 In mango smoothie bowls
3 Over quesadillas
4 In tacos
5 On grilled veggies
6 In canned fish salads
7 Over rice bowls
8 As a kick to dips & sauces
9 On chopped fruit or vegetables

Leche de tigre hot sauce

OK, bear with me on this one. I love Peruvian food; it's fresh, fishy, citrusy and packs the smallest yet most delectable kick that always surprises. One of my favourite dishes is ceviche: chopped raw shellfish or fish marinated in citrus and spices. The acid from the citrus cures the fish and gives it the perfect firm-to-soft texture and mouthfeel. I always find myself wanting to drink the fish-citrus mish-mash left over at the end, as it's completely addictive. Others must feel the same, because as it turns out, this bottom-of-the-bowl sauce is called *leche de tigre*: 'tiger's milk'.

As a fan of this marinade, I had to find a way to recreate it without needing raw fish... which is where this recipe comes in. In this completely untraditional hot sauce, I blend all the ingredients in the Peruvian marinade but, instead of curing raw fish with it, I just add a drop of fish sauce to round it out. It's absolutely gobsmacking and – I'm going to be honest – I'm still in awe that it works and tastes delightful. It's a citrus-forward hot sauce that starts out as tangy and acidic as you'd expect, but leaves you with both a ripple of chilli heat and sweet depth from the fish sauce.

WHAT YOU NEED

4 chillies
½ onion
1 garlic clove
1 nub of root ginger
    (or 2 tsp ginger paste)
sea salt
filtered water
1 tbsp fish sauce
juice of 2 lemons

WHAT TO DO

1   Follow the base How to make hot sauce recipe (see page 66), but add the ginger at the fermenting stage and the fish sauce and lemon juice at the blending stage.

PAIRING IDEAS

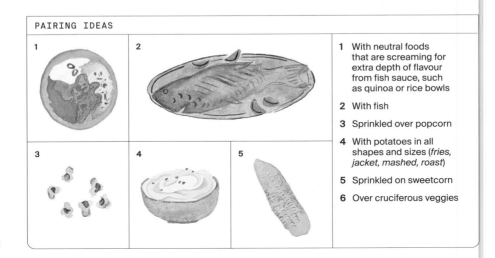

1   With neutral foods that are screaming for extra depth of flavour from fish sauce, such as quinoa or rice bowls

2   With fish

3   Sprinkled over popcorn

4   With potatoes in all shapes and sizes (*fries, jacket, mashed, roast*)

5   Sprinkled on sweetcorn

6   Over cruciferous veggies

Sweet n spicy hot sauce

If you want to get really crazy with this one, add a dollop of your favourite berry jam during the blending stage as well.

WHAT YOU NEED
2 red chillies
½ onion
sea salt
filtered water
2 red peppers
60ml ACV
80ml honey
berry jam (optional)

WHAT TO DO 1 Follow the base How to make hot sauce recipe (see page 66), but add the red peppers, ACV and honey at the blending stage, along with the berry jam, if you like.

```
PAIRING IDEAS
```

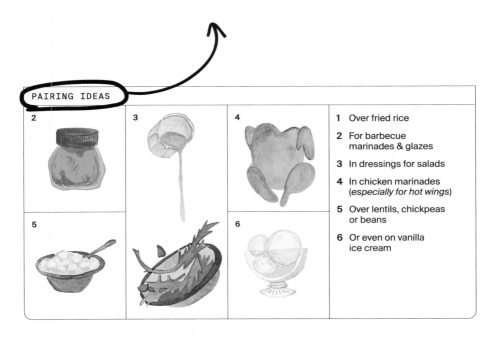

1 Over fried rice

2 For barbecue marinades & glazes

3 In dressings for salads

4 In chicken marinades (*especially for hot wings*)

5 Over lentils, chickpeas or beans

6 Or even on vanilla ice cream

Jalapeño & coriander hot sauce

I am a green hot sauce fanatic. Since anything green most likely means it's made with jalapeño, I'm sold. Jalapeños are low on the Scoville ranking, so they're milder chillies, which means you can drench whatever you're eating in this hot sauce without taking away from the essence of a dish.

WHAT YOU NEED

4 jalapeño chillies
½ onion
1 garlic clove
sea salt
filtered water
25g coriander

WHAT TO DO

1 Follow the base How to make hot sauce recipe (see page 66), but add the coriander at the blending stage.

ANYTHING GREEN OR WHITE!

↓

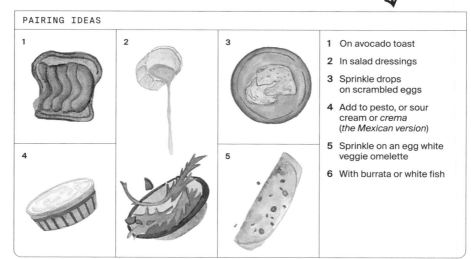

PAIRING IDEAS

1 On avocado toast

2 In salad dressings

3 Sprinkle drops on scrambled eggs

4 Add to pesto, or sour cream or *crema* (*the Mexican version*)

5 Sprinkle on an egg white veggie omelette

6 With burrata or white fish

Carrot & cumin hot sauce

Considering this is the **SPICY** section, it would be wrong to leave you without a hot sauce that *really* packs a punch. Not only do habanero peppers hit you with that intense, sweat-provoking, ear-ringing heat – ranking high on the Scoville scale with 100,000–350,000 SHU – but they're also the most beautiful orange hue.

WHAT YOU NEED

2 red chillies
2 habanero peppers
2 large carrots, chopped
½ onion
1 garlic clove
sea salt
filtered water
½ tsp ground cumin
¼ tsp ground ginger

WHAT TO DO   1   Follow the base How to make hot sauce recipe (see page 66), but add the carrots at the fermenting stage and the cumin and ginger at the blending stage.

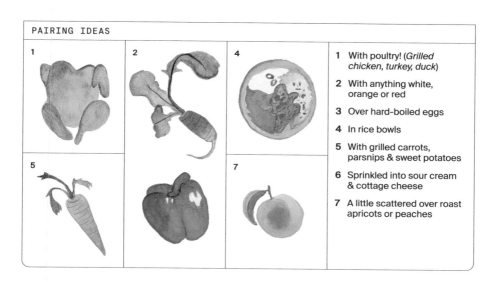

PAIRING IDEAS

1 With poultry! (*Grilled chicken, turkey, duck*)

2 With anything white, orange or red

3 Over hard-boiled eggs

4 In rice bowls

5 With grilled carrots, parsnips & sweet potatoes

6 Sprinkled into sour cream & cottage cheese

7 A little scattered over roast apricots or peaches

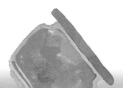

FRUIT IN JARS

JAM, JELLY
+ CHUTNEY

While I adore all condiments, it's those based on fruit and vegetables that I love making the most. Whether I am with my family in the French countryside using fruit from our trees, or in London at my tiny flat using four bruised pears that have been sitting for too long in my kitchen, there is no greater joy than making a jarful of jam.

(I would love to know why some people scoff at making just a jar or two of jam. The amount does not matter here, **there is no need to make hundreds of jars**! Quality over quantity.)

The beauty of jams, jellies and chutneys is that they allow us to taste a season past. There are few stronger emotions than those I feel when I am **tasting sunshine while staring at snowfall**. How magical is it to taste peaches in the dead of winter, or add quinces to a summer picnic? That preternatural feeling is available all year round from the right jar.

Sugar is a preservative, and, combined with fruit and veg, it preserves not only flavour but also seasonal essence, as well as reducing waste. Before I travel, I always make sure to finish up everything in my fridge, which usually involves an exciting mish-mash of tiny jars of jam and pickles.

Sterilising jars

To do this, simply wash empty jars and lids (for maximum hygiene, the lids should be new) in hot soapy water, then put them in an oven preheated to 130°C. While they only need around 10 minutes, I usually put them in once I start cooking the fruit for a jam, so they can sometimes be in there for closer to an hour, depending on what I'm making.

Since you're also cooking your jam until it reaches 104–105°C, its high heat will kill off any bacteria.

After filling the hot sterilised jars with the hot preserve, I flip the jars on to their lids. This both seals them and sterilises the lids once more from the inside.

Here's the thing: if a jar is sealed, looks great, smells appetising and has been stored in a cool dark environment, you're probably good to go. If there's any mould growth, toss it out! Further, the recipes in this book are for making minimal amounts, so it's likely you will have finished them before too much time goes by.

Rules of thumb

Sterilise your jars!

How to tell when jam or jelly is done

TEMPERATURE
The jam will reach 104–105°C

FREEZER TEST
I always keep a little saucer in my freezer for this. Just place a dollop of your supposed-jam on a cold plate, tilt the plate and see how slowly the jam trickles down. If it wrinkles when you push it back, it's ready

Fresh herbs

Any fresh herbs should be added **AFTER** cooking the jam and before jarring, otherwise their green colour will fade to brownish and look unappetising

Dried herbs

Any dried fruit or nut, vanilla pod, or dried herb or spice – such as chilli flakes, cardamom seeds or cinnamon – should be added alongside the fruit, sugar and lemon juice

¡!! Have FUN with it

Use vegetables, use fruit, or mix and match them

Practice makes perfect

What's in my jar?

Jam

Mashed-up
fruit + sugar

Marmalade

Citrus juice + its rinds + sugar

Preserves

Chunks of fruit
+ sugar. It's basically
just like jam, so don't
worry too much
about this one

Jelly

Purely fruit juice
+ sugar, no fruit chunks

Compote

A fruit 'sauce'.
Compotes are made
of fruit + sugar, slowly
cooked and not
preserved, such
as apple sauce.
A coulis falls under
this category, such
as raspberry coulis
on a chocolate cake

Fruit cheese

A dense paste made of fruit pulp + sugar.
There is no soft jellified texture: think of the
quince paste membrillo

Oh, but we aren't stopping with sweet jars. Let's get into the tangy and savoury world: Pickle? Chutney? Relish? These are a bit trickier to define.

SORRY, IT'S NOT MY FAULT!

Curd

Fruit juice + sugar + egg yolk. Usually made with citrus: think lemon curd

Pickle

Cut or full-sized vegetables or fruit in a salt or vinegar mixture. A pickle can be lightly cooked, but usually is not

Relish

Similar to a chutney, but usually only uses a single fruit or vegetable. In the US, a relish will have a firmer texture than a chutney, but in the UK, a relish tends to have a more liquid consistency... confusing, right? The perfect way to display this discrepancy is with a classic chunky US hotdog relish vs Ireland's prized Ballymaloe smooth tomato relish

Confit

Whole fruit (*sometimes pieces*) candied and fully infused to its core with sugar

Chutney

Just like jam, only add vinegar + spices and throw some veggies + alliums in there. Similar to a relish, but with a more viscous consistency, such as Indian mango chutney, or Branston pickle (*which is actually a pickled chutney*)

I hope I haven't confused you *too* much. Honestly, just call them what you like, there's no condiment police out there to get you. The terms will mean slightly different things between countries, due to each land's specific history. The trade routes and spread of their influence across borders is what makes condiments so fascinating! Yes, they're delicious, but their origins and the motives behind their inception are packed with cultural significance, too.

The beauty of simplicity is expressed in jam: fruit and sugar. Most guides to jam-making will imply you need kilos of fruit and access to equipment and supplies equal to those of the grandest country kitchen. This is – thankfully – untrue and it's causing you to miss out on the joy of sweet, sticky fruit made with as few as three apples.

History of jam

Though the first ever jam recipe was featured in the Roman cookbook *De Re Coquinaria* in 400 CE, it called for honey as the sweetening agent rather than sugar. It is likely that the Middle East was also producing jam at the same time, but made with sugar*. It wasn't until 1,000 years later, with the Crusades, that sugar was brought from the Middle East to Western Europe and from there sent around the globe. This boosted jam's popularity and helped make it easier to produce.

Both fruit and sugar were considered **rarefied luxuries**, which made the condiment fascinating and desirable to the public, but reserved solely for the elite. Louis XIV planted exotic fruit such as pineapples around Versailles as a way to boast about his widespread reach, travels and wealth. With these, he was able to serve unique jams on silver spoons when entertaining, in a display of power.

Further, the now-ubiquitous spread was meant to bring strength to anyone who consumed it: rumour has it that Joan of Arc would eat a spoonful of quince jam before going into battle. Nostradamus even published the 1552 *Treatise on Makeup and Jam*, a 'medical cookbook' with jam recipes to not only cure the plague, but also to attract love, or give you shiny blonde hair.

Nowadays, jam is one of the most popular condiments. I don't know whether the omnipresent sweet and seasonal spreads will make you strong, but they will surely **make you happy**.

---

* Sugar cane was first domesticated nearly 10,000 years ago in New Guinea, from where it spread to the Philippines and India. There, it was refined for the first time, then its journey extended slowly towards the West.

Pectin

How does jam gel? Please meet magical, naturally occurring pectin.

Simply put, pectin is a starch found within the cell walls of fruit and vegetables, which creates that lovely jam **shimmy and wobble**. Though you can buy it in powdered or liquid form at the shops, I prefer to rely on the pectin that comes from within the produce I'm using.

Every jam will – and should – be a different texture, because of differing fruit pectin levels. Apples and quinces are high in pectin and will produce a firmer set, whereas berries and cherries have low pectin levels and will produce a wobblier jam. This is OK! That's the beauty of homemade jam, there will be one for every occasion and personal preference. When combining different fruit, if you like a firmer set jam or jelly, be sure to include a high-pectin fruit. (Tossing in an apple is always easiest.)

Many people might be tempted to wait until their produce becomes extremely ripe and mushy to jar up its sweetness, but beware: this will lead to a less-set jam or jelly. Unripe produce has a higher pectin level than ripe fruit. My perfect mix of fruit is half unripe (for its pectin) and half ripe (for the taste).

Don't let the chart opposite scare you. Just because your favourite fruit has a low pectin level does not mean you should shy away from making jam with it. I don't mind a loosely set jam, as I think it celebrates the identity of its fruit and I accept them all as they come. For instance, I would now find a solidified apricot jam quite odd, as I have accustomed myself to this variety being looser, due to its medium pectin levels, with large, acidic chunks of fruit. To get the most out of natural pectin, my trick is to leave each fruit for as long as possible (twenty-four hours is ideal) macerating in sugar and lemon – citrus shells have the highest pectin content – as this process will extract the maximum jam gel from the fruit. I still get excited when I come back the following day to check on my macerated fruit and find it swimming in a glossy pool of sweet syrup.

Fruit pectin levels

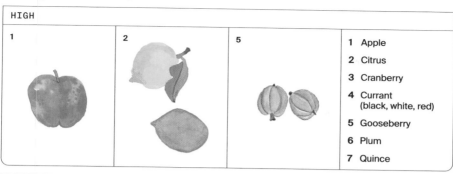

HIGH

1	2	5

1 Apple
2 Citrus
3 Cranberry
4 Currant (black, white, red)
5 Gooseberry
6 Plum
7 Quince

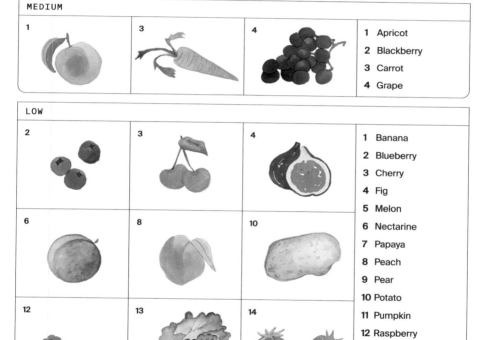

MEDIUM

1	3	4

1 Apricot
2 Blackberry
3 Carrot
4 Grape

LOW

2	3	4
6	8	10
12	13	14

1 Banana
2 Blueberry
3 Cherry
4 Fig
5 Melon
6 Nectarine
7 Papaya
8 Peach
9 Pear
10 Potato
11 Pumpkin
12 Raspberry
13 Rhubarb
14 Strawberry
15 Tomato
16 Watermelon

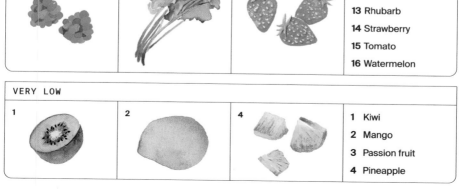

VERY LOW

1	2	4

1 Kiwi
2 Mango
3 Passion fruit
4 Pineapple

How to make jam

Simple steps, easy-to-grasp ratios, scale-able up or down, extremely versatile.

Since this is a template for a low-sugar jam, it won't keep as long as a shop-bought jar. Sugar is a preserving agent, so the less you use, the less time the jam will keep. You've still got a good six months minimum of preservation (and trust me, I have kept them for longer). Once opened, I recommend storing the jars in the fridge.

For extra-astringent and sour produce such as rhubarb, feel free to up the ratio to include more sugar; perhaps try a ratio of 2:1 fruit to sugar.

Here's the thing: you *can* rush jam, but you shouldn't. The longer you macerate the fruit in sugar and lemon, the gloopier, stickier and shinier your jam will be. That is why the only step here I urge you to follow is the twelve-hour minimum maceration in lemon and sugar, if you're using regular sugar (rather than jam sugar).

WHAT YOU NEED

fruit
white granulated sugar
lemon(s)
large pot (*it honestly doesn't need to be a specialised preserving pan*)
cooking thermometer
sterilised jars (see page 74)

WHAT TO DO

1 Peel the fruit, if you'd like. I peel fruit with cores such as apples, quinces and pears, but leave the skin on fruit with pits and smaller seeds such as apricots or plums. It's truly up to you.

2 Cut the fruit into pieces the size of your liking.

3 Weigh your fruit and add around one-third of its weight in sugar. Put both fruit and sugar into the large pot. This ratio is **SO** flexible, but since I don't like jam too sweet, I usually stick to it. I also like easy numbers so, if I have about 700g of fruit, instead of measuring out a perfect one-third of that (233.3g) in sugar, I'll usually add 250g.

4 Squeeze in the juice of 1 lemon (or 2–3 depending on your amount of fruit and preference for acidity). Throw the lemon shells in, too. Let the fruit, sugar and lemon sit in the fridge overnight.

5 Next morning, your fruit should have let out a lot of sticky liquid. This is fantastic: it will become the shiny jelly holding the jam together.

6 Place a small plate or saucer in your freezer.

7 Place your pot over a high heat and boil the jam for 20–30 minutes, removing the lemon shells after 5 minutes. Once the jam reaches 104–105°C on the cooking thermometer, it should be ready!

8 Take out your chilled plate, plop a bit of jam on it and tilt the plate. It should be thick and shouldn't run down the plate. If it does, feel free to keep it over the heat for longer to thicken it, or just jar it anyway! Liquid jam isn't bad jam, it's just a matter of texture preference.

9 Fill the sterilised jars with the jam, close the lids and flip over to seal. You'll hear pops from each jar over the next few hours.

PAIRING IDEAS

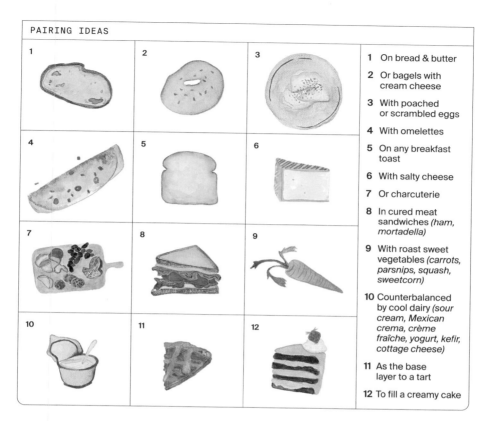

1. On bread & butter
2. Or bagels with cream cheese
3. With poached or scrambled eggs
4. With omelettes
5. On any breakfast toast
6. With salty cheese
7. Or charcuterie
8. In cured meat sandwiches (ham, mortadella)
9. With roast sweet vegetables (carrots, parsnips, squash, sweetcorn)
10. Counterbalanced by cool dairy (sour cream, Mexican crema, crème fraîche, yogurt, kefir, cottage cheese)
11. As the base layer to a tart
12. To fill a creamy cake

Once you have mastered this basic three-ingredient jam, feel free to add additional fruit, herbs or spices, change the sugar level and so forth. You'll see, it's shockingly easy, and in no time you'll be adding your entire fridge and kitchen cupboards to the pot. The beauty of making your own jam is that you can suit it to your tastebuds.

Jam isn't just for breakfast, it can and should be added to more than just bread and butter. To avoid the sticky, cloyingly sweet post-jam slump, just remember: jam is sweet and should be paired with something salty, or cool and creamy. By this, I simply mean to always think of jam as a rounding-out agent, the secret star of a dish that should amplify any and all flavours hitting your senses.

CONGRATULATIONS, YOU HAVE MADE JAM

Jam: the universal recipe

Traditionally, jam was made using a 1:1 ratio of fruit to sugar. Since sugar
is a preserving agent, a higher amount of sugar will result in a jam that keeps longer!
My formula calls for less sugar, so unless I am giving jars away to friends, I tend
to make smaller batches. Feel free to increase the amount of sugar to fit your
tastebuds and your preserving needs.

RATIO

To make jam

| Prepared, chopped fruit weight | × | 0.33 | → | This is your sugar amount |

WHAT TO DO

1 Add one-third of the total weight of the fruit in sugar.

2 Put the fruit + sugar + lemon + additional spices or dried herbs in a suitably sized saucepan.

3 Keep in the fridge overnight.

4 Bring to the boil, then keep stirring with a wooden spoon over a medium heat until the jam measures 104–105°C on a cooking thermometer, removing the lemon shells after 5 minutes. This should take 20–40 minutes depending on your chosen fruit's water content and the strength of your stove. (Or you can use a chilled saucer to test for a set, see page 82.)

5 Meanwhile, sterilise your jars (see page 74).

6 If you're adding a fresh herb, do so once the jam is ready.

7 Jar up your jam (see page 82) and enjoy!

YOU CAN MAKE ANY OF THESE VARIATIONS USING THIS FORMULA

FUN FLAVOUR VARIATIONS

1   Rhubarb-ginger
2   Blueberry-bay leaf
3   Gooseberry
    -lemon-elderflower
4   Peach-cinnamon
5   Nectarine-nutmeg
6   Apricot-thyme
7   Apple-clove
8   Green grape-Lillet
9   Red grape-mulled
    wine spices
10 Raspberry-mint
11 Guava-vanilla
12 Cherry-sage
13 Pineapple-
    peppermint
14 Carrot-
    mustard seed

Surprise strawberry jam

Strawberry jam is, and will always be, a huge crowd-pleaser. While it is perfect on its own, it continues to be wonderful when paired with exciting, unexpected ingredients. I urge you to play around with the recipe below. I have made this with parsley (1 tbsp), bay (1 leaf), chilli flakes (1 tsp), chopped mint leaves (1½ tbsp), chopped basil leaves (1½ tbsp), vanilla (1 pod), red wine (2 tbsp), Port (1 tbsp) and also combined it with any other berries I had laying around.

You really can't go wrong with strawberry, so whether you love a classic or want to bring some pizzazz to it, the world is full of empty jars waiting to be filled with enticing, unforeseen condiments. What memories do strawberries evoke in you? What is that moment you want to recreate with every spoonful?

500g strawberries
165g white granulated sugar
½ lemon

Just follow the How to make jam recipe (see page 82), adding any additional flavourings (see recipe introduction) at the optimal time (see page 84).

Pear & lemongrass jam

I rarely pat myself on the back with a flavour combination discovery, but I am extremely proud of this. One day, I was in the midst of chopping up some pears to make jam and remembered I had two ugly lemongrass stalks sadly withering away in my kitchen. I decided to plop them into the pears, lemon juice and sugar maceration pot because *why not?* The next morning, I ate a chunk of lemongrass-infused pear and, without exaggerating, my life was forever changed. I now love adding roast pears to anything I cook with lemongrass *(curries or fish)*.

500g pears
165g white granulated sugar
1 juicy lemon
1 lemongrass stalk

Follow the How to make jam recipe (see page 82), macerating the lemongrass alongside the pears, sugar and lemon. The lemongrass can also be subbed out for any herbs or spices you may like, adding them at the optimal time (see page 84).

A CLASSIC REVAMPED

OR PERHAPS TRY ONE OF MY OTHER FAVOURITE JAM RECIPES

PAIRING IDEAS	
1	1 With creamy soft cheese *(Brie, Camembert)*
	2 Or bagels & cream cheese
	3 With scrambled eggs
2	4 A dip for tortilla chips with honey mustard *(just try it)*

PAIRING IDEAS	
1	1 With blue cheese
	2 Alongside duck confit
	3 With grilled pork
2	4 Or grilled prawns
	5 With vanilla cake
	6 Or crêpes
7	7 Or croissants
	8 Dolloped on to Greek yogurt & pistachios

Fig & vanilla jam

My home in France is also home to five giant fig trees. Many of them give fruit twice a year, which just means we have a **LOT** of figs. Every August, despite eating more than fifty off the trees a day, pairing them with cheese, making tarts, cakes or baking them with wine, I always have so many left over. So as not to waste any fruit, I end up making *dozens* of jars of fig jam to bring back to London with me, to give to friends or enjoy once fig season is over. In the past, I've tried combining figs with different herbs and spices, but I personally prefer to keep the jam simple and enhance it only with a vanilla pod to bring out its warmth.

500g figs
165g white granulated sugar
1 juicy lemon
1 vanilla pod

Follow the How to make jam recipe (see page 82), macerating the scraped vanilla pod alongside the figs, sugar and lemon. I like to keep the emptied-out vanilla pods in my jars with the finished jam, as I find the flavour continues to infuse through it as the jar is eaten.

Tomato-vanilla-basil jam

I once had a tomato-vanilla jam in France, and it rocked my world. And no, not green tomato jam, but bright red tomato jam with specks of vanilla seeds throughout. For years, I went back to the shop where I bought it asking if they had any and no one there seemed to remember they had ever sold it. If I didn't vividly remember each spoonful of the jam, the chunky slathering of it on to baguette and butter, I would have thought I had gone absolutely mad.

Eventually I realised that enough was enough: it was time for me to make it on my own. After many recipe tests, I finally mastered the flavour I was missing. In classic Condiment Claire mode, I also took it a step further and tried adding basil to the mix. I now never make this recipe without the herb, but I've made it optional for you in case you're not quite there **yet** *(the 'yet' is important)*.

500g tomatoes (a mix of ripe in-season cherry or plum tomatoes and a couple of larger tomatoes)
165g white granulated sugar
1 juicy lemon
1 vanilla pod
2 tbsp chopped basil leaves

Follow the How to make jam recipe (see page 82), macerating the scraped vanilla pod alongside the tomatoes, sugar and lemon. Stir in the basil once your jam has reached setting point and you're ready to jar it up, so the leaves stay nice and green.

PAIRING IDEAS

1 With vanilla, coconut, lemon or carrot cake
2 Sandwiching Linzer cookies
3 As a dip for madeleines
4 In doughnuts
5 With cottage cheese or other fresh cheese
6 With Yogurt cake (see page 92–95)

PAIRING IDEAS

1 With any fresh soft white cheese
2 Or baguette and butter
3 Or crêpes
4 On a cake such as Yogurt cake (see page 92) with a dollop of crème fraîche
5 With cheesecake
6 With vanilla, stracciatella or fior di latte ice cream
7 With panna cotta
8 In a cake or biscuit

Now what?

Jam can be eaten whenever and wherever, as well as paired with hundreds of foods. After making myriad batches of jam and trying new varieties weekly since (almost) birth, I've come to realise that my ideal pairings are founded in colour:

DARK MEAT AND GAME
⟶   Dark purple / blue jam

1   Venison + blackcurrant jelly
2   Boar + plum jam
3   Pork + blueberry jam
4   Lamb + fig jam
5   Duck + elderberry jelly

LIGHT MEAT AND FISH
⟶   Orange jam

1   Chicken breast + apricot jam
2   White fish + mango jam
3   Guinea fowl + orange marmalade
4   Rabbit + rowan jam
5   Scallop + sea buckthorn jam

BEIGE FOOD

⟶ Pink or red jam

1 Mashed potatoes + cranberry sauce

2 Scrambled eggs + strawberry jam (every American knows that strawberry jam slathered on a breakfast platter will end up being mixed into eggs for a sweet pairing!)

3 Cottage cheese + cherry preserves

4 Sour cream + pickled red onions

ANYTHING GREEN

⟶ Not jam

1 Green beans + tapenade

2 Celery + vinegar pickle chutney

3 Endive + tzatziki

4 Cucumber + herbed salt

5 Fennel + honey mustard

1

2

3

4

1
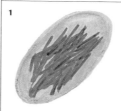

5

IT'S TIME TO THINK OUTSIDE THE BOX AGAIN. WHILE JAM IS WONDERFUL ON BREAD + BUTTER

IT'S ALSO A WONDERFUL ADDITION TO MUCH MORE. SUCH AS CHEESE

Stinkometer

GOAT'S CHEESE

CAMEMBERT

FETA

CREAM CHEESE

RICOTTA

BRIE

TALEGGIO

HALLOUMI

MANOURI

FRESH, SOFT WHITE

SOFT WHITE

SEMI-SOFT SALTY WHITE

LEAST STINKY

DARK, DEEP JAMS TO PAIR WITH SOFT FRESHNESS

SWEET JAMS TO PAIR WITH CREAMINESS

SWEET TO BALANCE THE SALT

FIG

BLUEBERRY

RASPBERRY

PEACH

HONEY

MEDLAR JELLY

CHERRY

GRAPE

APRICOT

STRAWBERRY

GREEK SPOON SWEETS (SUCH AS GRAPE)

TANGY SURPRISES

HERBY OR SPICY, FOR CONTRAST

TANGY

CRANBERRY

TAPENADE

CHILLI JELLY

CRANBERRY

BLACKCURRANT

BALSAMIC GLAZE

HERB JELLY

EARTHY

TAPENADE

HERB JELLY

OR SPICY, BUT NOT TOO SPICY

OR FATTY

CHILLI CRISP

HOT PEPPER JELLY

OLIVE OIL

CHILLI OIL

CHEDDAR

PARMESAN

GORGONZOLA

STINKING BISHOP

GOUDA RACLETTE

PECORINO MANCHEGO

STILTON ROQUEFORT

ÉPOISSES MUNSTER

HARD

SALTY HARD

BLUE CHEESE

STINKY

MOST STINKY

SWEET

SWEET TO BALANCE THE SALT BOMB

SWEETNESS TO CELEBRATE THE BLUE FLAVOUR

ACID TO CUT THROUGH THE STENCH

APPLE (FRESH, JAM, JELLY)

GREEN TOMATO JAM

HONEY APRICOT JAM

PEAR JAM GRAPE JELLY

CORNICHONS GREEN OLIVES

PEAR JAM HONEY

SPICY, OR SPICE-FORWARD

QUINCE JAM (MEMBRILLO) DATE

FIG JAM HONEY

MUSTARD

HOT HONEY CHILLI JAM

PLUM JAM PERSIMMON

BUTTER (DON'T JUDGE, JUST TRY)

ANY VINEGAR PICKLE

VEGETABLE CHUTNEY

TART TO CONTRAST

CHUNKY SOUR CHERRY JAM BLUEBERRY

PICKLED ONION

SPICY MANGO CHUTNEY

BLACKCURRANT

I LOVE AN ENDIVE WITH GRAPE + BLUE CHEESE COMBO

ALE CHUTNEY BLACKCURRANT JAM OR JELLY

WINE JELLY

RED FRUIT JAM OR JELLY

Yogurt cake
Gâteau au yaourt

When my yogurt cake recipe video went viral, I felt nothing but pure *guilt* because it's not my recipe. This is the first baking recipe any French child learns to make, their go-to dessert at the drop of a pin. It's simple, reliable and perfectly customisable. If any parents are reading, it's also mess-free: the only tool you need is an individual yogurt pot. It's best to find a 120–150ml pot because, though this is mostly based on ratios, it uses two eggs, so try not to use a pot that is too big or too small. If in doubt, try anyway! There's no harm in experimentation in the kitchen.

This is truly a French classic and one of my childhood favourites. I can remember four-year-old me sitting at the kitchen table as my ninety-year-old grandmother taught me. Its simplicity does not diminish its flavour, rather that gets sweeter with the years, as it embodies a nostalgia that is my personal Proust's madeleine.

Gâteau au yaourt is versatile and adaptable to any palate, so feel free to experiment with the recipe. You can eliminate the lemon and make a straight vanilla cake, replace the lemon juice and zest with that of an orange, or even swirl through your favourite jam (*lemon marries particularly well with raspberry or strawberry*) or spread (*chestnut purée or Nutella anyone?*) before baking.

Eat it plain, or top it off with your condiment of choice. I've even been known to toast a slice and spread it with soft salted butter.

WHAT YOU NEED

½ yogurt pot of neutral oil, plus more for the tin
1 pot filled with natural yogurt
2 pots of sugar
2 eggs
1 tsp vanilla extract
3 pots of plain flour
1½ tsp baking powder
pinch of fine sea salt
finely grated zest and juice of 1 lemon

WHAT TO DO

1   Preheat the oven to 180°C. Oil the loaf tin.

2   Place the sugar and wet ingredients *(oil, yogurt, sugar, eggs, vanilla extract)* in the bowl and mix thoroughly.

3   Add the dry ingredients *(flour, baking powder, salt)* and mix again.

4   Add the lemon zest and juice and do a final mix.

5   Scrape the cake batter into the prepared tin.

6   *If you'd like to swirl through some jam, feel free to do so here.*

7   Bake for 30–40 minutes.

8   Leave to cool. Serve plain, or top with any of my ideas (see right), or your own creations.

FOR YOGURT CAKE

FAVOURITE CONDIMENTS
TO SWIRL IN
1 Any jam or jelly. I find red versions look the best, so I usually opt for a raspberry, cherry or redcurrant
2 Try chocolate spread, chestnut purée, nut butter... you can't go wrong with this recipe
TO TOP
3 Lemon glaze (*icing sugar & lemon, so easy!*)
4 A spicy chocolate drizzle (*chocolate, cream, butter, cayenne & a pinch of cinnamon*)
5 Salty cinnamon sugar

YOGURT CAKE / GATEÂU AU YAOURT

INGREDIENTS

½ POT OIL

1 POT YOGURT

2 POTS SUGAR

2 EGGS

1 TSP VANILLA EXTRACT

3 POTS PLAIN FLOUR

1½ TSP BAKING POWDER

PINCH OF FINE SEA SALT

FINELY GRATED ZEST AND JUICE OF 1 LEMON

METHOD

1. MIX THE SUGAR AND WET INGREDIENTS (OIL, YOGURT, SUGAR, EGGS, VANILLA EXTRACT) THOROUGHLY

2. ADD THE DRY INGREDIENTS (FLOUR, BAKING POWDER, SALT) AND MIX AGAIN

3. ADD THE LEMON ZEST AND JUICE AND DO THE FINAL MIX

4. BAKE FOR 30-40 MINUTES AT 180°C IN AN OILED 900G LOAF OR CAKE TIN

5. LEAVE TO COOL, THEN SERVE

JELLY

I think of jelly as **the princess of condiments**: she's beautiful, shiny and must be handled carefully. Jelly seems like the most daunting of the sweet condiments, because of her stained-glass window-like, translucent appearance and jiggly texture. It's understandable to be daunted because, whereas an unset jam can still be used as a compote, an unset jelly is just a liquid mess.

Here's the main point to remember: the recipe for jelly is the same as jam, except it's made with fruit juice rather than chunks. As with jam, the jelly-making process takes some time, though in this instance you are not macerating the fruit, but cooking it and allowing it to drain overnight, extracting every bit of juice. You can't rush it, you have to just let the fruit do its thing all on its own, and you will be rewarded by a perfectly clear, beautifully set essence of fruit.

I find jelly is the best condiment to give as a gift, as there is nothing quite as magical as handling a jar of colourful, transparent, **suspended sweet juice**.

Since I want to make condiment-making as accessible as possible, I will start with the easiest jelly to make without additional 'help' from gelling agents such as agar agar or different gums. It is created by using high-pectin fruit. Apples, citrus, quinces, plums and tart berries such as gooseberries, cranberries and blackberries all fall under that category.

For ease, I'd recommend using either quinces or apples in the recipe over the page as the starting-off point on your jelly-making journey. Once you've become comfortable with this rewarding, wobbly, sweet-set condiment, you can venture towards adding low-pectin fruit to the mix and creating the jelly concoction of your dreams! And for my non-sweet-toothed readers, herb jellies are a fantastic way to impart a surprisingly tangy and fresh taste to any meal. The recipe in this section can be used for any herb, from classic mint to aromatic lemon verbena.

How to make apple jelly

Because they are naturally rich in pectin, unripe apples (or quinces if they are available in your area) are perfect for jelly. I like using Pink Lady apples due to their tartness, but use whichever your heart desires. Whatever apples you use, don't discard the cores: they have high levels of pectin and will help your jelly solidify.

WHAT YOU NEED

6 apples (about 900g total weight)
750ml water
white granulated sugar
juice of 1 lemon
largish saucepan

colander
muslin
large bowl
cooking thermometer
sterilised jars
  (see page 74)

YOU CAN SWAP APPLES OUT FOR QUINCES

WHAT TO DO

1 Chop up your apples (cores included) and place them in the largish saucepan. Cover with the measured water: your apples should happily float.

2 Turn the heat on and bring to the boil, then reduce the heat to a simmer. Cover and cook until very soft (30–40 minutes).

3 Line the colander with the muslin and place on top of the bowl. This is where you're going to collect the apple juice. Pour the saucepan contents into the muslin-colander contraption.

4 Let the apples sit overnight; they will slowly trickle all their juices into the bowl. Don't smoosh them down or squeeze the muslin, as this will make the liquid cloudy, just let them work their magic.

5 The next morning, weigh your apple juice, make a note of its weight, then pour it into the cleaned saucepan.

6 Add one-third of its weight (yes, like jam!) in sugar, then pour in the lemon juice. (Don't add the lemon shell.)

7 Boil, uncovered, until it reaches 104–105°C: like jam, this is jelly's setting point. Test for a set on a saucer, if you like (see page 82).

8 Place the jelly in the jars, flip them over and – just like that – you've got your first batch of apple jelly!

PAIRING IDEAS

1

3

6

1 On bread & butter
2 Or fluffy sweet pastries
3 As a cake filling
4 In a yogurt bowl
5 In a PB&J (see page 170)
6 With ham & pork

Double-whammy herb jelly

For my herb jellies, I cook the fruit with the chosen herb and add chopped-up leaves just before jarring for the visual effect; hence, the double-whammy herb punch. I had never had herb jelly before moving to the UK and I find it a great addition to a Sunday roast. For this recipe, stick with a neutral cooking apple such as a Bramley.

WHAT YOU NEED

5 cooking apples
(roughly 1kg)
5 fresh or dried herb sprigs
(I like using rosemary,
thyme or sage), **plus more
for jarring**
500ml water
250ml apple cider vinegar
(ACV)

white granulated sugar
juice of 1 lemon
largish saucepan
colander
muslin
large bowl
cooking thermometer
sterilised jars (see page 74)

WHAT TO DO

1 Chop up your apples (cores included) and place them in the saucepan with the herb sprigs. Cover with the measured water and ACV. Your apples should be somewhat submerged in liquid at this stage.

2 Turn the heat on and bring to the boil, then reduce the heat to a simmer and cover with a lid for about 25 minutes until soft.

3 Line the colander with the muslin and place on top of the bowl. Pour the saucepan contents into the muslin-colander contraption.

4 Let sit overnight; they will slowly trickle all their juices into the bowl. Don't smoosh them down or squeeze the muslin, as this will make the liquid cloudy, just let them work their magic.

5 The next morning, weigh your apple juice, make a note of its weight, then pour it into the cleaned saucepan.

6 Weigh out one-third of its weight in sugar and add it and the lemon juice to that same saucepan (not the lemon shell though).

7 Bring to a boil uncovered until it reaches 104–105°C. Once off the heat, add the chopped fresh herbs and stir through, then jar up.

OTHER GREAT HERB JELLIES

1 Quince & rosemary

2 Plum & oregano

3 Blackcurrant & mint

4 Apple & sage

Boozy jelly

While jellies are perfect for cocktail making, let me introduce you to **wine-as-jelly** as well. Jelly is the best condiment medium for wine, as the flavour isn't masked, the texture is light and it is punchy yet jiggly. There is nothing heavy about a wine jelly, but it excites the tastebuds with a zing of flair.

Also known as *gelée de vin*, wine jelly is a common condiment in France; I grew up making it with my family. In the Loire Valley region of France, a common dessert is *tarte vigneronne*, a simple apple tart with a stunning dark pink Chinon glaze painted on top. It's much simpler than it seems and the results always impress guests and add that extra oomph to any dish.

I know I said I wanted to make these recipes easy (and they are), but this needs a gelling agent. You can use agar agar, jam sugar, gelatine... I tend to use jam sugar as it is often easiest to find. Wine jelly tends to be served more liquid than a regular fruit jelly, so add more of your gelling agent of choice if you like a firmer set. The fun part about this recipe is you can swap in any bottle of wine (see opposite for more on this).

Bottle of wine jelly

WHAT YOU NEED

1 bottle of wine
gelling agent (use *one* of the below):
  12g (3 tsp) powdered pectin*
  OR **4g (1 hefty tsp) agar agar, or more for a more solid set***
  OR **If you prefer to use jam sugar instead, your jelly will be sweeter, as you will need 600–750g to get a set**
400g white granulated sugar *(do not add if you're using jam sugar)*
saucepan
whisk
sterilised jars

WHAT TO DO

1 Heat the wine in the saucepan and bring to the boil to burn off the alcohol. Add any extra spices in a spice bag now, such as cinnamon, cardamom, pepper and so on, if you'd like.

2 Optional: if you've chosen to infuse the wine, turn off the heat and let the saucepan sit for 10 minutes. Then remove the flavourings and return the infused wine only to the heat.

3 Add the pectin, agar agar or jam sugar. If not using jam sugar, add the white granulated sugar now too. Whisk to dissolve.

4 Bring to the boil, then continue to simmer for 5–10 minutes. It doesn't need to reach any particular temperature, and if you cook this for longer, the jam sugar will be too set and you'll have a stiff jelly.

5 Add to your sterilised jars, cool, then place in the fridge. Don't worry if the jelly doesn't look set, as it takes a few hours to take shape.

* *For any liquid, you will need three times as much volume of pectin for a set as you would of agar agar.*

PAIRING IDEAS

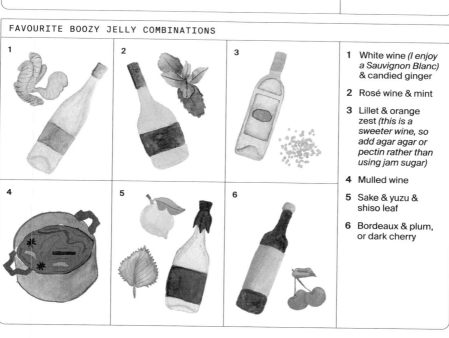

1 With red meat such as lamb, duck, terrine or pâté

2 Alongside poultry

3 As a glaze for a tart *(such as a tarte vigneronne with Chinon)* (see recipe introduction, left)

4 With creamy, salty hard cheese

5 As a sauce base

FAVOURITE BOOZY JELLY COMBINATIONS

1 White wine *(I enjoy a Sauvignon Blanc)* & candied ginger

2 Rosé wine & mint

3 Lillet & orange zest *(this is a sweeter wine, so add agar agar or pectin rather than using jam sugar)*

4 Mulled wine

5 Sake & yuzu & shiso leaf

6 Bordeaux & plum, or dark cherry

CHUTNEY

Chutney is one of my favourite condiments, as it is so **easy to make your own bespoke version** and it hits so many flavour notes. It's sour, it's sweet, it has texture, colour and myriad uses in different worldwide cuisines. The best part is, if you make your own chutney, you can personalise it with spices, fruit, vegetables, herbs, even different vinegars and sugars. My recipes are not authentic to India's native chutneys, but they are true to my tastebuds and to my love of seasonality. I prefer to use shallots rather than onions, because I find they give a rounded flavour (and less bad breath, to be completely honest), but feel free to tweak any of the recipes to include onion if that's what you have to hand, or enjoy more.

History of chutney

I could write an entire book on chutney, its influence and its shift across borders since it was invented in India more than 1,500 years ago. Much later, in the 18th century, the East India Company brutalised and dominated Indian territory, including expropriating their most culturally significant flavours, chutney among them. Once the East India Company began exporting foods to Britain, chutney's flavour impact began to take root in the West. There's something to keep in mind when you next see chutney on your local supermarket shelf.

Under the British Raj, the entire UK became even more infatuated with the **scrumptious sweet-and-sour condiment** and couldn't get enough. Eventually, British cooks began producing western-style chutneys using fruit and vegetables native to their *terroir**, which was much cooler than India's sweltering climate. The flavours of India were not exactly replicated, as the ingredients used were different; however, it gave us eaters two styles of delicious chutney, each used in distinct ways.

What all chutneys do have in common as a condiment group, though, is that their **acidity cuts through rich and fatty flavours**.

---

* Think of *terroir* as a place and environment with its own temperature, climate, soil, topography and so on. The term is commonly used to describe the location where a wine is produced.

How to make chutney

1   Boil vinegar with a sweetener (sugar, syrup, molasses and so on), salt, any spices and herbs and – usually – alliums (onions, shallots…). This step isn't necessary and you can skip it and add everything to the pan at once, but I prefer to cook the alliums first, as I find it gives the chutney less of a pungent onion flavour.

2   Once the alliums are translucent, add the remaining ingredients (fresh and dried fruit and vegetables and any alcohol).

3   Simmer over a medium heat for 30–40 minutes, stirring rather frequently, especially as time goes on.

4   Turn off the heat once your chutney is glossy and gloopy. You should be able to draw a line through the chutney with a wooden spoon and see the bottom of the pot.

5   Pot in sterilised jars (see page 74).

6   This is the toughest part: you need to let your chutney sit in a cool dark place for a minimum of 2 weeks after making it, to allow the vinegar to work its magic. After that time, you can open the jar, but once it's popped open, remember to keep it in the fridge. It will keep for a few months, or for a single evening filled with lots of cheese, wine and laughter.

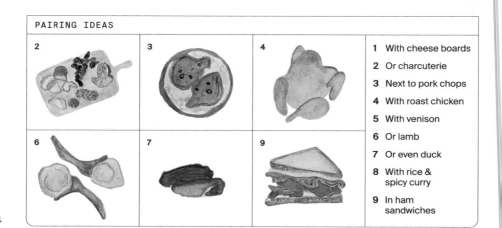

PAIRING IDEAS

1   With cheese boards
2   Or charcuterie
3   Next to pork chops
4   With roast chicken
5   With venison
6   Or lamb
7   Or even duck
8   With rice & spicy curry
9   In ham sandwiches

The four seasons of chutney

Pinky spring chutney

Pink rhubarb,
Pink Lady apple, cranberry,
strawberry & shallot

60ml apple cider vinegar (ACV)
60ml white wine vinegar
125g white sugar (*demerara also
works, but it darkens the colour*)
pinch of salt
10g root ginger, finely grated
1 large shallot (80g), sliced
250g rhubarb, chopped
**1 Granny Smith apple (80g), cored
and chopped**
230g strawberries, sliced
25g dried cranberries

Peachy summer chutney

Sweet pepper & peach
(with no alliums)

240ml ACV (*any other white
vinegar also works*)
100g white sugar
100g demerara sugar (*or white
sugar, for a clearer colour*)
½ tsp salt
2 tsp mustard seeds
1 tsp ground ginger
3 thyme sprigs
3 red or yellow peppers
(total weight 315g), **chopped**
4 peaches
(total weight 400g), **chopped**

Spicy autumn chutney

Spicy plum & Port

300ml any white vinegar
200g carob molasses
100g brown sugar
pinch of salt
3 tsp mustard seeds
1 tsp chilli flakes, or more to taste
1 cinnamon stick
½ tsp ground ginger
1 onion and 1 shallot
(total weight 175g), **sliced**
800g plums (weight before
pitting), **pitted and chopped**
2 tbsp Port

Cosy winter chutney

Apple, cinnamon
& raisin

100ml ACV
60ml malt vinegar
150g white granulated sugar
pinch of salt
1 cinnamon stick
1 onion (100g), sliced
5 tangy apples, *I tend
to use 4 Granny Smiths
and 1 rogue Royal Gala*
(total weight 470g),
cored and chopped
30g sultanas

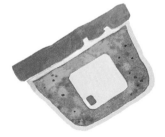

PICKLES + FERMENTS

A SAVOURY WAY TO
PRESERVE: QUICK PICKLES,
SAUERKRAUT, KIMCHI,
MISO, PONZU ↪

Spot the difference

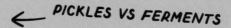
← PICKLES VS FERMENTS

While most of us know and love them, have you ever wondered what it really means when goods are described as 'fermented' or 'pickled'? They're not the same thing, but both are delicious and they can be tricky to differentiate. Have no fear, I'm here to help you understand!

When an ingredient is pickled, some sort of acid has been added. This just means that it's been placed into an acidic brine to achieve the signature mouth-puckering sour flavour. On the other hand, a fermented food has had no acid added to it: instead, the sourness you taste is due to a chemical reaction occurring within the fermented ingredient. This reaction is very commonly achieved using salt, but it is possible to ferment with other ingredients as well.

Pickles

A pickle uses a vinegar (*acetic acid*) brine, which instantly creates the tang we crave. Pickles sadly have no probiotic benefits, they're just quite delicious. The vinegar protects your ingredient of choice from spoilage. Pickles don't need to be kept in the fridge until they're opened

Quick pickles

These also use acid, aka vinegar, in their brine and they are my absolute favourite go-to pickles. They're quick to make and created for short-term storage: simply heat up a brine, pour it over any vegetable or fruit in a jar, put in the fridge immediately and enjoy within a few hours and up to a few weeks

PICKLED HERRINGS, PICKLED VEGETABLES (ONIONS, CARROTS AND SO ON)

Fridge = ferment, shelf = pickle

Fermented foods are 'alive', full of probiotics and need refrigeration, whereas pickled foods are 'dead', have little nutritional benefit and their vinegar brine protects them from any bad bacteria, so they are shelf-stable.

You may be wondering: are all gherkins pickled? Well, that depends on their preparation. If you find them sold in a jar with an acidic brine containing vinegar, they are pickles; if they come in a salt brine, they are fermented. Check the back of your favourite jars: it's always interesting (and useful) to know what you like best.

OLIVES, CAPERS, DILL PICKLES, BEER, WINE, YOGURT + SAUERKRAUT, KIMCHI, SOURDOUGH, KOMBUCHA

Ferments

Fermented foods have been transformed due to microorganisms, and require a salt brine and good bacteria to activate and nurture the fermenting process. Good bacteria already present on the skins of fruit and vegetables – the most common being *lactobacillus*, aka your everyday healthy gut probiotic – produce the lactic acid required for fermentation when they break down the sugars of the produce. (*It's the lactic acid which gives the tangy flavour to ferments.*) And these good bacteria just love a salty environment. Bad bacteria, serendipitously, loathe salt, plus they hate the sour living conditions provided by lactic acid. So you salt-brine your ingredient of choice, weigh it down, keep it at a constant temperature and *voilà*. Ferments are not shelf-stable long-term, but, after about a week, just put them in the fridge and enjoy. Moreover, fermented foods contain living organisms, help strengthen our intestinal flora, preserve vitamins and are well digested by most people

PICKLES

In the same way as for fruit in jars, pickles are condiments that allow you to **carry produce into different seasons** by means of preservation. The longevity of these goods has helped people sustain themselves during the winter for millennia, simply by eating summer's bounty in a jar.

History of pickles

The first mention of pickles in literature appears more than 9,000 years ago in a Chinese manuscript. Initially a tool to conserve foods during harsh months for the working poor, pickling spread across not only classes but also geographical borders. The pickle had mass appeal, infiltrating the world due to its addictive taste and signature snap and mouthfeel. Further, many diverse methods of pickling appeared regionally. Depending on what preserving agents were available, different regions used these to create their distinct cultural 'pickle markers'. For example, in Peru they pickle fish using primarily citrus juice rather than vinegar and they call this ceviche (see page 68).

America was literally named after a pickle dealer. You're thinking: *Claire, wasn't it named after the Italian explorer Amerigo Vespucci?* You are correct! On top of being the first explorer to circumnavigate the American continent, he was also Christopher Columbus's pickle dealer. As a ship handler, Vespucci provided Columbus with pickles for his journey across to the Americas for the first time. They were supposedly so delicious that, once Columbus found he needed to return to Europe, he demanded that cucumbers be planted in Haiti to ensure he'd have a supply of pickles for his journey home.

How to make a quick pickle brine

I love quick pickling. Full stop. Also known as refrigerator pickling, this process is just an easy, fast way to achieve the **tangy flavour and snappy texture** of your dream pickle. When quick pickling, all you need to do is create some sort of vinegary brine, chuck it in a jar with your chosen fruit or veg, seal it up and toss it in the fridge. Wait a few hours and you've got yourself a pickle!

Some of my favourite quick pickling recipes include pickled red onions, radishes, apples, persimmons, grapes... there are genuinely too many to name. I tend to stick with a base brine for both vegetables and sweeter fruit. Feel free to play around with your vinegars of choice, as well as with herbs, spices and so on.

RATIO

To make a quick pickle

Equal parts 5% acetic acid vinegar $+$ Water $\rightarrow$ A quick pickle

NOTES

Toast any spices you use! This will enhance all your flavours.

Play around with vinegar combinations.

Think about colour: apple cider vinegar (ACV), malt vinegar and soy sauce will all darken a mixture.

CHECK YOUR VINEGAR LABEL SAYS 5 PER CENT ACIDITY

Pay attention to the ratio above. If using soy sauce – which tastes great but only has one per cent acetic acid – rice vinegar (four per cent and quite a staple in my household), or fresh herbs (due to their water content), these will all dilute the vinegar brine, so you'll need to add more vinegar, to balance the quick pickle ratio above.

WHAT YOU NEED

240ml vinegar *(50:50 white and ACV is always nice)*
240ml water
1 tbsp sweetener: sugar, maple syrup or honey
1 tbsp salt
sterilised jar (see page 74)
saucepan

Optional extras that take this basic brine to the next level (see right and overleaf, too)
½ tsp mustard seeds
¼ tsp chilli flakes
2 peppercorns
1 clove
1 bay leaf
1 garlic clove

WHAT TO DO

1 Pack your jar with vegetables and/or fruit of choice.

2 Heat the brine ingredients (vinegar, measured water, sweetener and salt) in the saucepan, with any optional extras, until the sweetener has fully dissolved. Bring to the boil.

3 Turn off the heat.

4 Pour the hot brine over the veg or fruit of choice in the jar, close the lid and pop into the fridge.

5 Wait a few hours and feel free to enjoy for up to 2 weeks.

SOME OF MY FAVOURITE QUICK-PICKLE DUOS

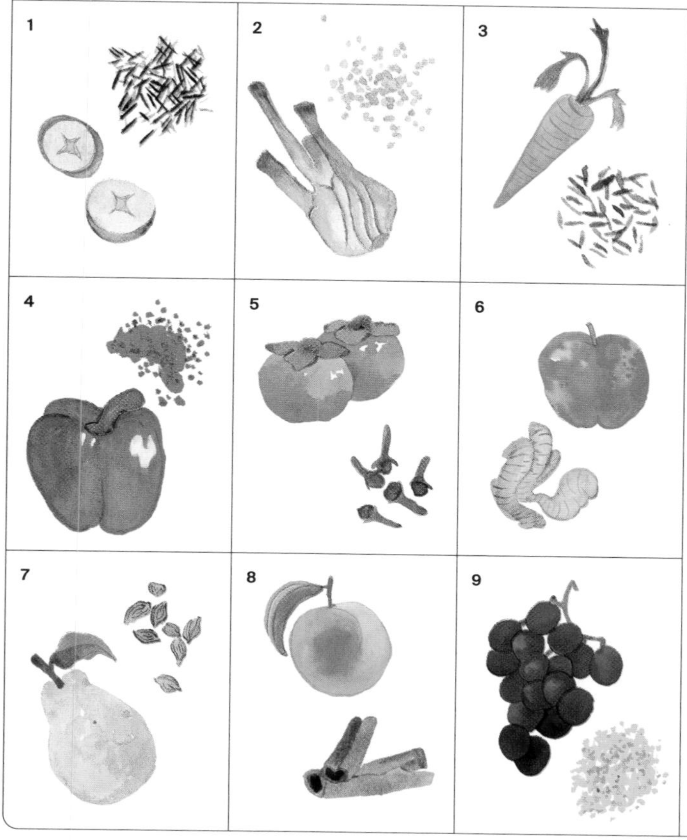

1 Cucumber & dill

2 Fennel &
mustard seeds

3 Carrot & caraway
seeds

4 Red pepper
& chilli flakes

5 Persimmon
& cloves

6 Apple & ginger

7 Pear & cardamom

8 Apricot & cinnamon

9 Grape & lemon zest

SPICES AND DRIED HERBS (AND OTHER THINGS) TO TRY IN QUICK PICKLES

1 Caraway
2 Cardamom
3 Celery seeds
4 Chilli flakes
5 Cinnamon sticks
6 Cloves
7 Fennel seeds
8 Ginger
9 Mustard seeds
10 Pepper
11 Dried herbs, alliums or citrus zest
12 Bay leaves
13 Dried dill
14 Garlic
15 Grapefruit, lemon or orange zest
16 Onions

Quick pickled red onions

Straight out of college, when I lived in NYC, I had a weekly Friday evening date with red onions before meeting up with my friends. These pickles have been a hit among my loved ones for *years* and I'm embarrassed (but also proud) to admit they used to be my entire personality. My trick for these onions is to boil them in the brine, to make sure you get rid of the onion aftertaste. You only place them in there for a bit, so they keep their delicious crisp bite. No risk and all reward.

The splash of soy sauce here really makes a difference and brings out the sweet depth of the red onions.

WHAT YOU NEED

4 red onions
240ml water
240ml white vinegar
120ml ACV
1 tbsp rice vinegar
1 tbsp soy sauce
1 tbsp sugar
1 tsp salt
mandoline (optional *but appreciated*)
saucepan
sterilised jar (see page 74)

WHAT TO DO

1 Thinly slice your onions, or run them through the mandoline.

2 Add these with all the other ingredients to the saucepan (*yes, you're boiling the onions with the brine*).

3 Bring to the boil, then reduce the heat and simmer for around 3 minutes (*the onions will become translucent*).

4 Turn off the heat and jar up! These quick pickles will keep for 1 month, if not longer.

PAIRING IDEAS

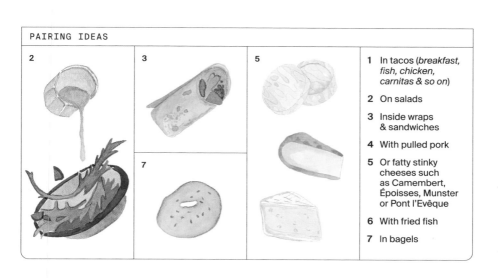

2

3

5

7

1 In tacos (*breakfast, fish, chicken, carnitas & so on*)

2 On salads

3 Inside wraps & sandwiches

4 With pulled pork

5 Or fatty stinky cheeses such as Camembert, Époisses, Munster or Pont l'Evêque

6 With fried fish

7 In bagels

Quick pickled mustard seeds

Think of these as vegan caviar. Providing little bursts of tangy brine to brighten up heavy dishes, pickled mustard seeds are unexpected dinner party heroes and can be made in just under an hour.

WHAT YOU NEED

40g yellow mustard seeds
120ml ACV, plus 1 tbsp
1 tsp maple syrup (*you can use honey or sugar as well, brown sugar will taste great, but the colour will change*)
½ tsp ground ginger
½ bay leaf
pinch of chilli flakes
½ tsp salt
sieve
bowl
saucepan
small sterilised jar (see page 74)

WHAT TO DO

1   Rinse the yellow mustard seeds in the sieve and drain well.

2   Put your seeds in the bowl with the 120ml of ACV and let sit to get to know each other for 30 minutes.

3   Put these plumped-up seeds and their vinegar in the saucepan along with the remaining ingredients (but reserve the extra 1 tbsp ACV).

4   Bring to the boil, then reduce the heat and simmer for 15 minutes.

5   Put them in the jar, top with the extra splash of ACV, stir and seal.

6   Place in the fridge. They will keep for 1 month.

```
PAIRING IDEAS
```

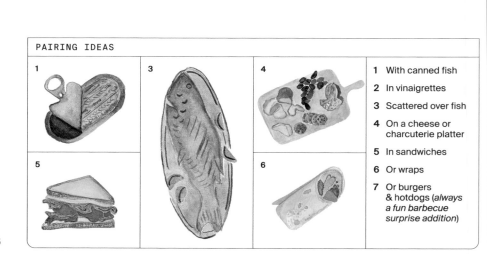

1   With canned fish

2   In vinaigrettes

3   Scattered over fish

4   On a cheese or charcuterie platter

5   In sandwiches

6   Or wraps

7   Or burgers & hotdogs (*always a fun barbecue surprise addition*)

Bread-and-butter quick pickles

If you're feeling adventurous, have some time and want to venture into 'real' pickling, these pickles are for you. Ever wonder where that name came from? During The Great Depression in America, a common lunch was a sandwich made of these sweet, sliced cucumbers in between slices of buttered bread. They were great at distracting from the taste of subpar sandwich meats, too.

WHAT YOU NEED

1 cucumber
½ onion
1 tbsp salt
360ml any white vinegar
100g white sugar
1 tsp mustard seeds
½ tsp fennel seeds
1 clove
¼ tsp chilli flakes
bowl
sieve
sterilised jar (see page 74)
saucepan

WHAT TO DO

1   Slice the cucumber and half onion and place in the bowl. Toss them both with the salt. Cover and place in the fridge for a good 2 hours.

2   You'll notice that they gave off a lot of water; drain this off and rinse in cold water in the sieve. Drain very well and place in the sterilised jar.

3   In the saucepan, combine the vinegar, sugar and spices and bring to the boil, then reduce the heat to a simmer and cook for 1 minute.

4   Pour the brine over the vegetables, close the lid and allow them to come to room temperature.

5   Place the jar in a dark, cool place and wait at least 72 hours before enjoying. Once opened, store these pickles in the fridge and enjoy for up to 2 months.

PAIRING IDEAS

1   On their own as a snack
2   On burgers
3   Or hotdogs or toasties
4   With canned fish
5   In salads
6   Or sandwiches
7   Use the brine in a martini, salad dressing or marinade

NOW BACK INTO
THE WORLD OF

FERMENTS

While making your first ferment may seem intimating, I should warn you that, once you begin, it will become very difficult to stop. The fizzing of a ferment and the initial pop when burping a jar (see page 66) will become a healthy addiction. Apologies in advance to your soon-to-be overburdened kitchen work tops and stuffed-full shelves, as they will be filled with ever-multiplying fermenting crocks.

Fermenting is sort of like raising a baby. You must take care of it, and yes, burp it, until it develops into an adult.

Essentially, fermentation is the chemical breakdown of an ingredient. In this metabolic process, microorganisms such as **yeast and bacteria eat carbohydrates** (*the starch and sugar in the fresh produce*) and convert them into acid or alcohol. No air should touch your ingredients during fermentation. When in these conditions, and paired with the perfect environment, the ingredient you wish to ferment will begin to break down and become slightly effervescent.

Though it has become trendy in the past few years, due to its health benefits, fermentation is an ancient practice and there are ferments from all over the world that teach us a lot about each culture. Through fermentation, you can access not only new flavours but also **new vitamins and other nutrients** that didn't exist in the fresh produce.

The act of fermenting also gives ingredients a second life, by changing not only their texture but also their taste. A fermented fruit or vegetable will maintain its crisp outside but soften up in the centre and then unleash a world of tang upon your first bite. There's a whole secret world within each fermented item that takes time to come to life. In fermenting, patience is truly a virtue.

Fermenting is both a science and an art, so your ingredient measurements will need to be precise to let loose its shapeshifting magic.

SALT +
WATER +
VEGGIE +
TIME =
DELISH
FERMENT

How to make sauerkraut

While sauerkraut is associated with German cuisine, due to its popularity in that country, its origins are probably Chinese. Around 2,000 years ago, the Chinese began shredding cabbage and adding rice wine to preserve the vegetable during the barren months. Also called *choucroute* in French and popular in the Alsace region, this delicious ferment has spread worldwide due to its taste and health benefits.

WHAT YOU NEED
1 cabbage (850g before cutting)
1½ tbsp (24g) **salt**
big bowl
sterilised jar (see page 74)

 ITS SOUR TASTE + STRINGY TEXTURE MAKE IT A PLAYFUL CONDIMENT

WHAT TO DO

1 Remove a large cabbage leaf and set it aside. Also remove and set aside the core and stalk end in a single piece.

2 Shred the remaining cabbage leaves and put them in the big bowl.

3 Add the salt and massage with your hands for about 1 minute.

4 Let sit for 30 minutes.

5 Come back to your bowl and mash the cabbage with your hands.

6 Pack the cabbage firmly into the jar, getting as much air out as you can. Leave room at the top, as bubbles will make the contents expand.

7 Top with the reserved large leaf and press firmly down. Add the heavy cabbage core and stalk and press down again.

8 Loosely place the lid on the jar.

9 Over the next day, press down the sauerkraut whenever you walk past it and make sure it's staying submerged (*you can also add fermenting weights to the top, if you'd prefer*).

10 Keep it at a constant temperature (*ideally around 21.1°C*). I always shove it in a dark cupboard.

11 After 1 week you should be good to go and enjoy! Keep the jar in the fridge once opened, for up to 6 months.

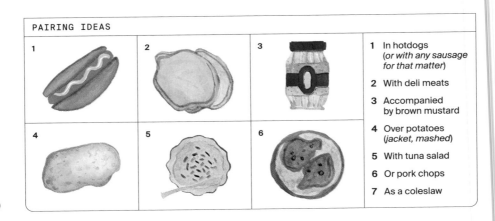

PAIRING IDEAS

1 In hotdogs (*or with any sausage for that matter*)

2 With deli meats

3 Accompanied by brown mustard

4 Over potatoes (*jacket, mashed*)

5 With tuna salad

6 Or pork chops

7 As a coleslaw

Fermenting rules of thumb

Temperature

Feel free to start eating your ferment within a week if it's hot outside *(more than 21°C)*; anything cooler than that and your ingredient may take more than two weeks to ferment

Salt brine percentage

2–5 PER CENT

I like sticking to no more than 2.5–3 per cent of the total produce weight in salt, as any higher and I find the salt overpowers the flavour of the vegetables or fruit. *(And this matters more when fermenting lighter-tasting produce, such as persimmons)*

Covered or uncovered ?

When you close the lid of a ferment, you allow both for carbonation and the production and storage of carbon dioxide. If your lid is semi-open or uncovered, your ferment won't be as fizzy, because the carbon dioxide will escape. There's no right or wrong, it's merely a matter of preference

Kimchi

Now that you've mastered sauerkraut, let's take it a step further with kimchi! Kimchi is an extraordinary condiment that incorporates all the taste notes: salty, sweet, sour, bitter and umami. In Korea, kimchi is **on the table at all times** as a condiment and no meal is complete without it. With its tangy, pungent flavour and crunchy texture, it is used to cleanse the palate in between bites. It is also incorporated into many of the country's iconic dishes, such as *kimchi bokkeumbap*, *jjigae* or *mandu*.

It uses a base of (usually) cruciform vegetables and salt, which goes to show not only that every country has their own method of vegetable fermentation, but, once again, that flavour is so culturally specific.

In Korea, there is almost always a spread of side dishes on the table, known as *banchan*. These fall into three larger categories: seasoned green vegetables, braised or soy sauce-based dishes, and preserved or fermented *banchan* such as *kimchi*.

Most fascinating, however, is the cultural marker that kimchi as a condiment represents: centuries of familial and cultural tradition. It's much more than delicious, fermented cabbage, it's **a way of life**.

Yearly, *kimjang* takes place. A 2013 addition to UNESCO's Representative List of the Intangible Cultural Heritage of Humanity, the making of kimchi transcends social classes and brings people together. This November celebration is much more than fermenting for sustenance during harsh winter months, but is rather a communal activity. Over *kimjang*, friends and family cooperate and create forever bonds over the condiment. It allows for sharing among all, using natural resources. Even though *kimjang* takes place in November, the entire process can last a year: seafood is obtained in spring, salt procured in early summer, fruit harvested and chillies dried and ground in late summer, and finally the big event takes place in the late autumn to make sure every household will have kimchi over the winter. It is a beautiful display of the human collective. A form of civic pride.

Kimchi has many variants, which add gochugaru chilli powder, spring onion, garlic, radish, spices such as ginger and even seafood. The kimchi you're probably visualising in your head right now is *baechu* (cabbage, or Chinese leaf) kimchi; however, the condiment differs across Korea due to distinct natural conditions. Koreans have learned to adapt to their unique geographical regions, environment and climate to produce kimchi uniquely and distinctly theirs. By the coasts and on islands, seafood-heavy kimchis are more popular. In the centre of the country, more herbs and vegetables go into the ferment, whereas in the colder regions, more meat and less chilli is used. Additionally, since kimchi is such a marker of identity, there are numerous recipes that have been passed down which are unique to nuclear families.

So, I promise, **there is a type of kimchi for everyone**. Don't like chilli? Don't worry! There is *nabak kimchi* (water kimchi). The chilli pepper didn't arrive in Korea until the 1500s and, even though we visualise kimchi as a red, gochugaru-heavy version, the first use of chillies in the ferment was only documented in the late 1700s. Don't like cabbage? There is *oi sobagi* (cucumber kimchi) and *kkakdugi* (radish kimchi) to name just a couple. I strongly suggest doing a deep-dive on kimchi through exploring any local or online Korean stores and restaurants.

The recipe over the page is for *mak* kimchi, which translates as 'careless' kimchi. It is the quick and easy version of *pogi* kimchi, the more arduous traditional method in which the head of cabbage is quartered. When making *pogi*, the supply is meant to last all winter, so a very large batch is made. The recipe overleaf is different, as I want you to explore flavour and **travel effortlessly via your tastebuds** in your own kitchen. In this smaller-batch *mak* kimchi, you chop up the cabbage, which reduces its fermentation time. The flavour won't be as intense as *pogi*, but it hits the spot when that kimchi craving strikes!

Kimchi combines all the elements that create flavour, including community and history, as well as remarkable taste.

How to make kimchi

Most recipes for kimchi will tell you to create a starch paste out of sweet rice flour: this binds the ingredients together and makes for a quicker fermentation time. I've found that the recipe here does the trick for me without needing to dirty another dish, so this is just my method. You can also blend the radish into the spicy paste, but I prefer it in chunks.

You could try adding an Asian pear or apple to the kimchi paste, or chopping it up alongside the other vegetables. This gives your kimchi a nice sweetness and promotes further fermentation, because of the sugar content. My friend's grandma uses any fruit she has lying around, even grapes. And if you want a more pungent, briny flavour, add oyster or raw shrimp to the paste, too.

This recipe can last you months, but, if you're like me, this jar should be gone within a few weeks (if not days).

WHAT YOU NEED

1 head of Chinese leaf (1–2kg)
65g Korean salt, or coarse salt, plus ½ tsp
cloves from 1 head of garlic
1 nub of ginger (to give 1 tbsp when blended)
2 tbsp fish sauce
1 tbsp shrimp paste
½ onion

35g gochugaru (*this is quite hot, so adjust depending on your liking for spice*)
3 bunches of spring onions
120g Korean radish, or daikon, julienned
60g carrots, julienned
large bowl
colander
gloves (*you don't want spicy eyes, I promise*)
airtight container, such as a sterilised jar (see page 74) **or airtight food container**

WHAT TO DO

1 Remove the outer layer of Chinese leaf and set aside.

2 Cut the remaining head of Chinese leaf into quarters, then into 5cm chunks. Place in the large bowl. (You'll be using this bowl to mix everything later, so make sure it's big enough!)

3 Add the 65g salt and toss with your hands. Let sit for 4–6 hours, allowing for the moisture to seep out of the leaves. Whenever you walk by (ideally every 15–30 minutes), toss the mixture again.

4 Rinse the Chinese leaf in the colander 3 times (my Korean friend's mum swears by this number, so just do it), to remove any salt, then let it drain for 1 hour. When well drained, replace in the clean bowl.

5 Blend the kimchi paste mixture together: the garlic, ginger, fish sauce, shrimp paste, onion, ½ tsp salt and – most importantly – the gochugaru.

6 Chop the spring onions and add to the drained Chinese leaf bowl with the julienned radish and carrots.

!! 7 **PUT ON YOUR GLOVES** and add your pungent, bright red paste to the vegetables. Massage through until every leaf is coated.

8 Place your new homemade kimchi (*exciting!*) into the airtight container and top with the layer of leaves you set aside, to create a barrier. Here you can also add clingfilm or baking parchment on top.

9   Let this container sit somewhere dark and cool for 24–48 hours. Keep tasting it. Do you like the flavour? Once you do, place in the fridge ready for whenever your heart desires. In the fridge, kimchi can last up to 6 months; at room temperature, it will continue to ferment and only last 1–2 weeks.

PAIRING IDEAS

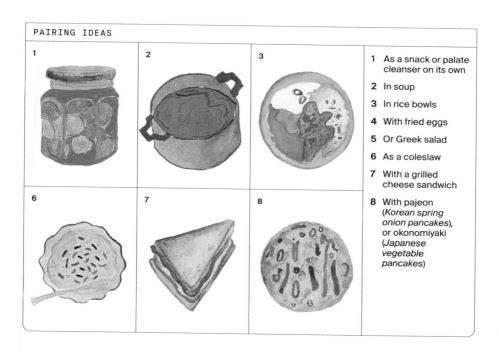

1   As a snack or palate cleanser on its own

2   In soup

3   In rice bowls

4   With fried eggs

5   Or Greek salad

6   As a coleslaw

7   With a grilled cheese sandwich

8   With pajeon (*Korean spring onion pancakes*), or okonomiyaki (*Japanese vegetable pancakes*)

Pickles & ferments around the world

1 EGYPT

Sourdough: fermented wheat and wild yeast was first invented here

2 THE CAUCASUS

Kefir, a fermented milk drink

3 HAWAII

Poi, pounded and (sometimes) fermented taro root

4 USA

Dill kosher pickles

5 RUSSIA

Kvass, a rye bread drink

6 UKRAINE, POLAND, RUSSIA

Borscht, made from fermented beetroot juice

7 ITALY

Giardiniera: pickled or fermented vegetables

8 FRANCE

Cornichons, crème fraîche (fermented cream)

9 ENGLAND

Worcestershire sauce, made with fermented alliums

10 TURKEY AND THE MIDDLE EAST

Tursu / torshi: fermented vegetables

11 ICELAND

Hákarl, fermented shark

12 SWEDEN AND DENMARK

Pickled herring

13 FINLAND

Viili, fermented milk with a thick, elastic texture

14 NORWAY

Lutefisk, dried cod fermented in lye

15 KOREA

Kimchi, (see page 122–125) doenjang, gochujang: fermented cabbage, soy bean paste, chilli paste

16 JAPAN

Gari (ginger), natto (soy beans) takuan (daikon), miso (soy beans again), kyuri zuke (cucumbers)

17 CHINA

Li hing mui (plum powder), pao cai, kombucha (fermented tea), doubanjiang (broad beans)

18 PHILIPPINES

Atchara (fruit or vegetables), balao balao (cooked shrimp), puto lanson (fermented rice cake)

19 VIETNAM

Nem chua: cured fermented beef

20 INDONESIA

Acar (fermented fruit or vegetables), tempeh (a soy bean cake)

21 THAILAND

Sriracha (fermented hot sauce), khanom chin (fermented thin rice noodles)

22 GERMANY

Sauerkraut (see page 120)

23 INDIA

Mango pickle, appam (fermented rice pancakes), idli (fermented rice and lentil cakes)

24 GHANA

Fufu (fermented cassava)

25 NIGERIA

Ogiri, a flavouring made from fermented oil seeds, such as sesame seeds and melon seeds

26 ETHIOPIA

Injera, a fermented pancake made from teff flour

27 WEST AFRICA

Sumbala (fermented locust beans), kenkey (fermented cooked maize dough)

28 MOROCCO

L'hamd markad: preserved whole lemons

29 MEXICO

Escabeche (fermented vegetables), atole agriole (masa-based drink of fermented maize)

Miso

There is nothing like a Japanese umami journey. With each bite, your entire body is struck head-to-toe with thousands of flavours, each varying in taste, prominence and duration. The art of mastery – *shuhari* – is evidenced in Japanese cuisine. This is a concept which originally stems from the martial art of *aikido* and directly translates as 'follow the rules, break the rules, transcend the rules'.

Shu 'follow', obey the rules

Ha 'move', break away from the rules

Ri 'individual path of transcendence', **be** the rules

This way of life is embedded within Japanese culture and evidenced in the country's food world through flavour. I am fascinated by the concept and, while I admire all masters of their craft, my gateway to understanding different cultures is through food.

So, to miso, a fermented soy bean paste. Its depth of flavour is matched by its dense and geographically varied history.

Its predecessor originated in China around 300 BCE and is referred to as *jiang*. Though initially made with fermented fish, meat and grains, soy beans took predominance around 200 BCE, as the supply was bountiful. It was only in the 7th century that the paste arrived in Japan from mainland Korea. At the same time, the Japanese Buddhist Emperor Tenmu banned farmed meat consumption*, which encouraged the eating of soy as a protein replacement. (This pescatarian, soy-heavy era lasted until the late 1800s and has left its mark on the country's modern diet.) Miso became a staple in Japan's larder, the **daily meal for samurais** during the Kamakura period in the 13th century, and an instant soup for combatants during the Japanese civil wars. It helped military commanders subsist when other food sources were scarce.

Though I focus on miso here, there are numerous fermented soy bean pastes around the world, such as its Chinese predecessor *douban jiang* as well as Korean *doenjang*. Further, depending on its maturation time, miso can range in pungency and colour from light to dark red. The longer you let miso mature, the deeper in colour it will become and the more pungent its taste and aroma.

* But not game, as the nobility enjoyed hunting.

Years ago, when I first took a stab at making miso, I was pleasantly surprised by how simple and straightforward the process was. Not only are there minimal ingredients, but the effort level is also low. Ever since, I have experimented with different legume blends and fermentation times and the results have each been **delectable in their own funky way**.

While I'm not claiming the recipe overleaf is perfectly authentic, it is my simple, home kitchen-friendly way to create an umami punch at home. It's how I've managed to learn more about Japanese flavour and yet stay as true to traditional methods as possible. You don't need many tools to make my miso, you just need time.

Please do not be intimidated by its long fermentation journey, as the reward is immense. I have made miso several times in the past decade, and it is **without a doubt the most satisfying homemade ingredient** to use while cooking. When I moved to the UK from the US, my saddest goodbye was to my miso.

Miso is that last puzzle piece that was missing for so long and that you've just discovered under the table. It's a condiment that **unites salty and sweet** and combines seamlessly with so much. It's perfect with most sweet goods, such as bananas, in any bakes, when roasting granola or with peanut butter, or I love making compound miso-maple butter for eggs, rice, bread and roast vegetables. What I'm trying to convey is that, just because a condiment serving suggestion isn't conventional or traditional, doesn't mean it can't work for you.

IT'S OK IT FOUND A GREAT HOME AND WAS THOROUGHLY ENJOYED

How to make miso

Miso is much easier to make than soy sauce (see overleaf). All you need are soy beans, rice koji and salt. I have experimented with many different legumes (*I am a fan of a 50:50 chickpea and soy bean combination*) but, for the purposes of this book, I will refrain from deviating too far from tradition.

If you've never heard of koji – the ingredient that activates the miso fermentation – it's a type of mould culture that is grown on rice, sweet potato, barley, soy beans and more. It can be used to produce not only miso but also soy sauce and sake. For my recipe, I use rice koji, but feel free to use whichever you'd like. While you can make koji, by inoculating your host product of choice with *Aspergillus oryzae*, I buy it. It's quite difficult to find even in Japanese food shops, so I get it online.

The liquid byproduct of miso, tamari, is gloriously thick and happens to be gluten free... The name stems from the Japanese verb *tamaru* which means 'to accumulate' (as the liquid does in the miso). Tamari is an ideal substitute for soy sauce (*shoyu* in Japanese), especially if, like me, you are drawn to a more velvety and rich texture. Only minimal amounts excrete during the miso fermentation, which teaches you to savour every droplet of it and give the ingredient the respect it deserves.

You know by now that I love a good ratio. The easiest way to make a miso is by using a 1:1 soy-to-koji ratio. Personally, I prefer using a tad more koji than soy, as it gives a sweeter flavour. If this is confusing to you, use a 1:1 ratio. Like most of the rest of the condiment world, there are no rules to miso making. The hard bit is the waiting.

WHAT YOU NEED

265g dried soy beans
300g shop-bought rice koji (or see recipe introduction)
around 90g salt, plus 1 tbsp
big bowl
saucepan
kitchen gloves (optional)
fermenting crock, glass or clay vessel
high-ABV alcohol, such as vodka, to clean the crock

WHAT TO DO

1   Soak the beans in double their volume of water overnight in the bowl.

2   The next morning, cook your beans in the saucepan in that same soaking water for 2–3 hours, or until soft to the touch.

3   Strain the beans over the big bowl, reserving the bean juice. Set aside 240ml of this bean juice (*don't sweat it if it's less*).

4   Weigh your soy beans and make a note of their weight.

5   Mash the beans until soft. You can blend them, but I prefer to have texture in my miso when fermenting. Mix in the reserved bean juice.

6   Add the koji and mix.

7   Calculate the salt you will need: 10 per cent of the combined total weight of the koji and cooked beans (it should be around 90g).

8   Put on your gloves and mix by hand (*optional but fun*). It's time to pack it up!

9   Wipe down the inside of your crock with vodka to make sure there is no bacteria. Line the base with around 1 tbsp salt.

10 With your hands, start forming tennis ball-sized lumps of miso and then throwing them down into the crock. This will reduce the amount of air pockets formed, and is a great way to release frustration! In between each tennis ball smackdown, make sure to pat each ball flat. Your goal here is to pack everything as tightly together as possible, to avoid an environment where mould can flourish.

11 Once all your miso is packed in, cut out a perfect circle from baking parchment and place it on top.

12 You're going to want to weight this down. I like to put a cardboard cutout sealed in a ziplock bag on the baking parchment, followed by a firmer item on top such as pie weights, fermenting weights or even a Tupperware full of water.

13 Close the crock and set aside for 6–12 months; the waiting time is up to you after that. The darker the miso becomes, the more pungent and richer the flavour.

14 After it has been sealed for 2 weeks, you should see some liquid pooling at the top: this is tamari. Congrats, you've made 2 condiments with 1 recipe! Open up your crock, collect this liquid and set it aside in a cute little bottle, or savour immediately. Close everything back up the way you found it and *try* to be patient until you can finally harvest more liquid gold. I recommend keeping it in an airtight container in a cool dark place once opened. I keep mine in the fridge to make sure it remains cool enough to preserve it. I've never had a miso go bad, but I would recommend enjoying it for up to 1 year.

NOTES

Try not to worry about any white mould! If you see some, just scrape it off and let the miso do its thing. If the mould is black, though, discard the entire batch.

Ideally, make miso during the winter, as the fermentation begins slowly due to low temperatures – creating more depth of flavour – and there is less humidity in the air. Full disclosure: I have made miso during the summer; it works and takes less time to ferment.

My method is adapted from many, including oral Japanese recipes (where I learned about sweet vs salty miso and koji ratios), Brad Leone (who taught me the brilliant ziplock cardboard cutout trick) and from *The Noma Guide to Fermentation*. Noma chefs use an exact ratio (3:2) of dried yellow split peas to koji for their 'peaso'. At the height of my fermentation obsession, I went to see a talk by David Zilber – then Noma's head of fermentation – and had a chance to ask him a question. Turns out, all my brain wanted to know right then was the grossest thing they'd ever fermented at Noma. It was blood.

Soy sauce

You may be wondering: *but Claire, what about soy sauce? How can I make this staple fermented condiment at home?*

When you grab a bottle from the supermarket shelf, you rarely think about the amount of work that was put into it. Your soy sauce, a constant in your kitchen, comes from thousands of years of tradition and labour, **exceptional mastery** and love.

I am not including a soy sauce recipe in this book because, while it is feasible to make at home, it does require extra-delicate steps – as well as a warm environment such as a fermentation chamber – which aren't quite as user-friendly as making miso. Please appreciate the level of detail and many steps from the (very simplified) chart opposite.

One of the **oldest sauces** in the history of mankind, soy sauce was originally used as a way to stretch salt. Like miso, this liquid condiment has Chinese origins that spread across Asia and eventually into the West. There are numerous types of soy sauce, as well as differing names for the condiment, as it spans the globe in thin and thick forms as well as dark, light, sweet and salty.

Though soy sauce is the perfect match for any Japanese dish – it is meant for dishes such as beautifully sliced sashimi, slightly warm nigiri and so forth – its magic does not stop there.

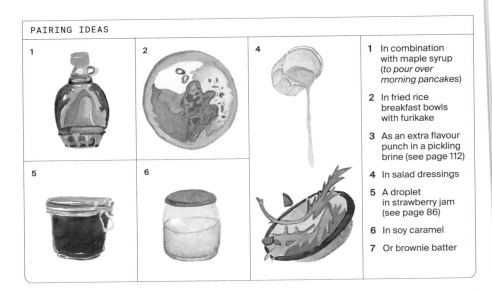

PAIRING IDEAS

1 In combination with maple syrup (*to pour over morning pancakes*)

2 In fried rice breakfast bowls with furikake

3 As an extra flavour punch in a pickling brine (see page 112)

4 In salad dressings

5 A droplet in strawberry jam (see page 86)

6 In soy caramel

7 Or brownie batter

How to make soy sauce

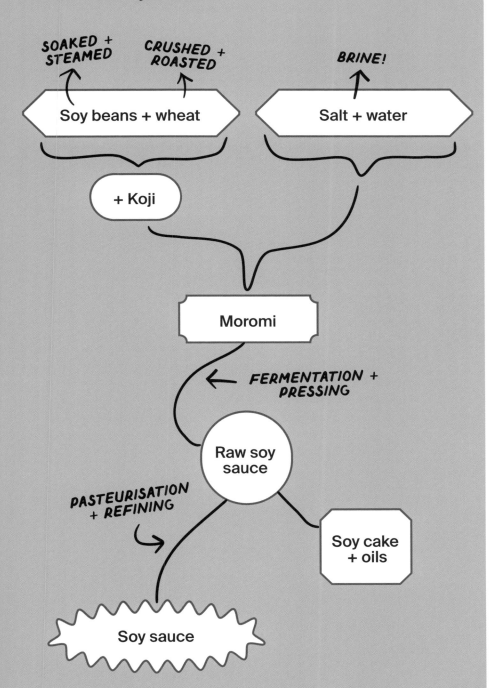

SOAKED + STEAMED

CRUSHED + ROASTED

BRINE!

Soy beans + wheat

Salt + water

+ Koji

Moromi

FERMENTATION + PRESSING

Raw soy sauce

PASTEURISATION + REFINING

Soy cake + oils

Soy sauce

Ponzu

Soy sauce is not only used as a condiment, but also as an ingredient. So here is how to make a condiment out of a condiment… **meta**. Ever heard of ponzu? Yes? Well did you know its name comes from a Dutch word? Invented in the 17th century, ponzu can be distinguished as *pon*, 'punch' in Dutch, and *zu* or *su*, which means 'vinegar' in Japanese. During this era, The Dutch East India Company was the only Western establishment invited to trade with Japan, as the country was still isolationist. The easiest way to describe ponzu is as a citrus vinegar. You could even say a mix between fruit punch and vinegar… see what I did there?

One of my favourite weeknight dinners is silken tofu with spring onions and ponzu. It's shockingly simple and yet, years after I started eating it multiple times a week, it is still exciting and just as satisfying. I crave it incessantly when I am travelling.

WHAT YOU NEED

120ml soy sauce
60ml citrus juice *(I like a mix of lemon, lime and clementine, or, if you can find yuzu, that makes a fantastic addition)*
120ml mirin
80ml rice wine vinegar
1 piece of kombu
6g katsuobushi (bonito flakes)
bowl
saucepan
sieve

WHAT TO DO

1   Combine the soy sauce and citrus juice in the bowl.

2   In the saucepan, combine the remainder of the ingredients and bring to the boil. Turn off the heat and let cool for around 15 minutes.

3   Once cooled, add the citrusy soy sauce and mix.

4   Strain this through the sieve and you've got yourself some ponzu!

5   Serve immediately, or keep in the fridge. Though ponzu can keep for years, this bottle will most likely be empty quite quickly.

PAIRING IDEAS

1
2
3

4
5
6

7
8

1 Drizzled on silken tofu
2 With raw prawns
3 Or scallops
4 In tuna salads
5 In a vinaigrette
6 With watermelon chunks *(even frozen)*
7 With sliced Pink Lady apples
8 With grapes
9 As a dipping sauce for cold noodles
10 With gyoza

DRESSINGS

VINAIGRETTE, CAESAR,
RANCH, FLAVOURED OILS

Good salad dressing has the addictive power to force your fork back into the plate even before you've finished chomping down on the previous bite. Though 'dressing' today is mainly used and thought of in this way – as a unifier of leaves to render a dish a 'salad' – it has many more uses than we tend to credit it with. Our ancestors knew this much better, seemingly, than we do. The first ever salad dressing is attributed to ancient Babylonia more than 2,000 years ago and was composed solely from oil and vinegar. Flash-forward to the time of European monarchies and royal chefs were known to combine around thirty ingredients to make complex dressings for fish and potatoes, for instance, as well as just for lettuce leaves. There is nothing quite like a crisp salad drenched in delicious dressing, but **don't keep it solely for leaves**. A drizzle on a beautiful slice of ricotta toast? In a bowl as a crudité dip? To level up basic sandwiches? You name it.

I like a 2:1 oil-to-vinegar ratio, because I like a bite to my dressing. If you prefer a calmer dressing, increase the oil element to 3:1 or even 4:1. As for the binder, seasoning and optional sweet, herb and extra punch elements (see opposite), those are entirely up to you. A dollop of this, a pinch of that... Play with your tastebuds and with the ingredients you have in your fridge. What pairing intrigues you? Try it out and learn about your preferences.

While we are going to start with the fundamental vinaigrette dressing, we will also go beyond the obvious into more modern creations.

What is a salad dressing?

NECESSARY
OIL + ACID + BINDER + SEASONING

OPTIONAL
SWEET + HERBS + EXTRA PUNCH

Oil

Olive, avocado, rapeseed, sesame, sunflower, walnut

Acid

Vinegar (*apple cider vinegar or ACV, balsamic, white or red wine, or rice wine*), citrus juice

Binder

Mustard of choice (*Dijon, honey, grainy*), mayo, tahini, nut butter, miso (see pages 168 and 130), anchovy paste, dairy (*yogurt, sour cream, Parmesan*), egg yolk

Seasoning

Salt, pepper, garlic and onion (*very finely chopped or in powdered form*), chilli flakes, cumin, paprika

Sweet

Brown sugar, fruit juice (*OJ, grapefruit, blackcurrant*), honey, jam and jelly, maple syrup, soy sauce

Extra punch

Caper brine, olive brine, pickle brine, finely chopped anchovies, finely chopped shallots, citrus zest, jalapeños, ponzu (see page 134), spring onions, Worcestershire sauce

Herbs

Basil, dill, herbes de Provence, oregano, parsley, thyme

Vinaigrette

I've come to realise that all my friends have different salad dressings, depending on where each is from. I love it when I'm visiting their homes for a meal and discover *their* dressing of choice, because it always indicates a little bit about their culture. I am a proud salad lover and so I have explored many different dressing iterations... but my at-home go-to always ends up being my Mamie Jeanne's vinaigrette.

The French have conducted a long-standing love affair with vinegar. Because of France's predominance in the wine world, the supply has been bountiful for hundreds of years. Wine was transported by the Loire River when making its way up to Paris for distribution and was tasted around the city of Orléans, which lounges on said river. Though bountiful, not all wine was tasty, but the unremarkable bottles were not tossed out, rather they were transformed into vinegar. The oldest method of making vinegar – called the 'slow process' – stems from the original Orléans method, in which wine, vinegar and a vinegar 'mother' are placed in wooden barrels and left to rest, work their magic and become a mouth-puckering condiment. Vinegar production was so commonplace in the region that, in 1394, *vinaigriers* (vinegar-makers who used the Orléans method) created their own corporation. In the 18th century this had 300 members, but today there is only one: Maison Martin-Pouret.

Due to this long history, it is unsurprising that the French adore their vinegar as both a patriotic symbol and a flavour staple. If you go to France, you'll most likely taste a version of vinaigrette at some point, as it's a staple at any home or café. You will find that, though it is nothing fancy, it just **pairs well with everything**, especially according to French Dijon-loving tastebuds.

Though it's never actually measured out, each household has a different oil-to-vinegar ratio. As I was recording the recipe opposite for the first time for this book – actual amounts have never been required before – I realised that my ratio of choice goes back to the lunches my grandma would make me as a child. There was nothing like landing back in France, after a twelve-hour flight from Los Angeles, driving three hours straight to her home and sitting down for lunch with a big plate of roughly chopped tomatoes, slathered in her vinaigrette.

How to make Mamie Jeanne's vinaigrette

This uses a 2:1 oil-to-vinegar ratio as well as quite a bit of Dijon, so it packs a punch! The standard vinegar used is a white wine or red wine vinegar, but I do love swapping either out for a balsamic occasionally.

The most important step in making this is to taste it! Do you want more of a vinegary kick? Add more. Too acidic for your liking? Add more olive oil. You can also (judiciously) choose to add any herbs, alliums or spices of your choice.

WHAT YOU NEED

60ml wine vinegar, or to taste
120ml olive oil, or to taste
1 hefty tbsp Dijon mustard, or to taste
pinch of salt, or to taste
½ garlic clove, very finely chopped (optional)
½ shallot, very finely chopped (optional, but highly recommended)

WHAT DO TO

1 Combine the vinegar, oil and mustard and give it a nice stir with a fork or whisk to emulsify it as much as possible.

2 Add the salt, garlic and shallot, if using, and give it a final stir.

3 Taste it and adjust the balance of all the ingredients to your liking.

4 If there is any left over, keep it in the fridge and enjoy it for up to 1 week if you've added garlic and shallot, or months if you haven't.

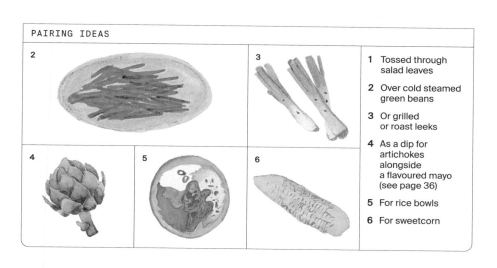

```
PAIRING IDEAS
```

2

3

4

5

6

1 Tossed through salad leaves

2 Over cold steamed green beans

3 Or grilled or roast leeks

4 As a dip for artichokes alongside a flavoured mayo (see page 36)

5 For rice bowls

6 For sweetcorn

Caesar and ranch

Though I am French, I did grow up in America, which means I have a soft spot for traditional American flavours. What screams America more than caesar and ranch dressings? You tell me. Unfortunately for my nostalgic cravings, I live in London, where it's difficult to get my hands on a respectable shop-bought form of either of those. Fortunately for you, I have mastered the at-home versions.

Caesar dressing

Caesar salad and its dressing were invented in Tijuana, Mexico. Yep, you read that right, caesar salad is from Mexico. The name is attributed to Caesar Cardini, an Italian immigrant who, alongside his brother Alex, ran a restaurant – Caesar's – in the 1920s. The restaurant was a huge hit with Americans, who were able to cross the border into Mexico and thus escape the Prohibition rules by car... It was frequented by big Hollywood stars (Clark Gable and Jean Harlow, to name a couple) as well as other icons, such as Julia Child. Supposedly, the dish was first called Aviator salad, as Alex Cardini had been a pilot in WW1. Shortly after, it was renamed Alex-Caesar Cardini salad after both brothers, then eventually shortened to 'caesar salad'. All this history is debated, but we *can* agree on the fact that it's absolutely delicious.

While the original recipe called for Worcestershire sauce rather than anchovies, as a canned fish aficionado, mine includes both. The best part about this is that it's a blender recipe. Just chuck all your ingredients in and *voilà*, you've got yourself a creamy, salty, smooth dressing!

WHAT YOU NEED

5 anchovies, or 1½ tsp anchovy paste
1 garlic clove, or ½ tsp garlic paste
3 tsp Dijon mustard
1 egg yolk
juice of 1 lime
1 tsp ACV
1 tsp Worcestershire sauce
35g Parmesan cheese, finely grated
60ml neutral oil (*olive oil works too but its flavour will be pronounced, it's a matter of preference*)
blender

WHAT TO DO

1   Place all the ingredients in your blender.

2   Blend! It's as easy as that.

3   If you have any left over, keep it in the fridge and consume within 3 days.

PAIRING IDEAS

1

2

3

4

6

8

1 In a turkey
   & grape wrap

2 Or a burger

3 On tomato-
   caper salad

4 Or grilled
   sweetcorn

5 Stirred into
   pasta salad

6 Mixed with peas
   to make a mash

7 As a marinade

8 Mixed through
   coleslaw

*THINK OF CAESAR
DRESSING AS THE
SALTY-UMAMI
ELEMENT OF A DISH*

Bright ranch

Had I not included a ranch recipe in this book, I think my American passport would have been revoked... But I wouldn't dream of skipping it, as I am a ranch **FAN**. There's '4am ranch', and then there's make-at-home bright ranch. In my opinion, '4am ranch' should come out of a crusty plastic bottle and be slathered on to a random kitchen saucer. It should be used for aggressively dunking a takeaway jalapeño-Hawaiian pizza between every bite. *If you're snarling at the thought of this, then I am sorry you haven't made your best memories with friends on the kitchen floor in the early hours.* Bright ranch, on the other hand, is lighter, tangier and herbier than your classic shop-bought brand, perfect for crudité dippage or spreading in sandwiches and the ideal counterbalance to anything fried and extremely spicy. There's a time and a place for everything, even ranch.

HISTORY

The origins of ranch dressing may be one of my favourite food history anecdotes... The tangy, creamy condiment was invented in 1949 by Steve Henson, a plumber. While working in Alaska, Henson would consistently make buttermilk dressing for his coworkers and it was a huge hit every time. (Buttermilk dressing had been popular among cowboys for decades, as buttermilk was common on the High Plains.) Flash-forward five years and Henson and his wife had moved out to California, bought a ranch (see where we're going here?) and named it Hidden Valley. Yep, the famous-in-America Hidden Valley ranch dressing brand. Though the couple began selling their famous buttermilk dressing to local supermarkets, it wasn't until as late as 1972 that they sold the name and the recipe – a simple combination of buttermilk, mayo and herbs – to the huge Clorox company for $8m.

My recipe is extremely inauthentic, as I am missing two of the three Hidden Valley ranch ingredients: buttermilk (*I know, I know*) and mayo. I find that the easiest way to recreate their creamy tang at home is simply by using low-fat Greek yogurt, as its texture is thin enough and it has the right acidity.

WHAT YOU NEED

220g low-fat Greek yogurt
120g sour cream
1 tbsp lemon juice
½ tsp ACV
2 tsp Worcestershire sauce
2 tbsp chopped chives

1 tbsp chopped dill
1 tbsp chopped parsley leaves
1 tsp garlic paste, or 1 garlic
    clove, finely grated
¼ tsp onion powder
pinch of salt and pepper

WHAT TO DO

1 Combine all the above and stir! Easy peasy.

2 If you have any left over, keep it in the fridge and consume within 3 days.

PAIRING IDEAS

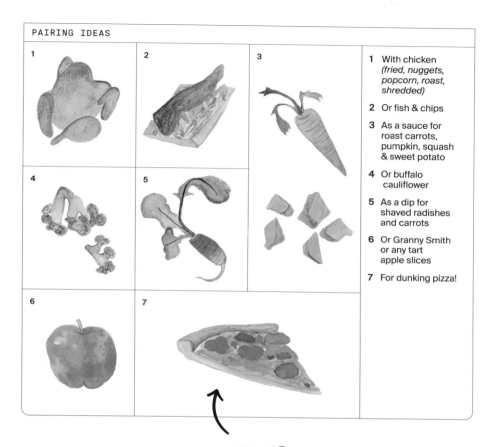

1 With chicken *(fried, nuggets, popcorn, roast, shredded)*

2 Or fish & chips

3 As a sauce for roast carrots, pumpkin, squash & sweet potato

4 Or buffalo cauliflower

5 As a dip for shaved radishes and carrots

6 Or Granny Smith or any tart apple slices

7 For dunking pizza!

TRUST ME:
LIFE-CHANGING

How to make flavoured oils

There is no need to spend an outrageous amount of money on flavoured oil, as it's ridiculously easy to make at home in just a few simple steps. While I like using a lighter extra virgin olive oil as the base, any neutral vegetable oil works as well.

I'd recommend making a small batch of any of these, keeping them in a cool dark cupboard and using them up within two months, as homemade infused oils don't keep as long as the processed shop-bought type.

WHAT YOU NEED
fresh or dried herbs, or garlic, or chilli or chilli flakes, or citrus zest
light olive oil, or neutral oil
mortar and pestle, or plastic bowl and rolling pin
sterilised jar and bottle (see page 74)
saucepan
sterilised metal funnel (see page 74, optional, *but useful*)
sterilised metal sieve (see page 74)

WHAT TO DO

1 Pick your herbs, fresh or dried, or other flavourings.

2 If you choose fresh herbs, wash them. Remember that oil and water repel each other, and that bacteria needs water to grow, so make sure to let them dry thoroughly before using. This is key.

3 Once you have your dried herbs, or other ingredients, smash them a bit to release their flavour. A mortar and pestle is good for this, or a sturdy plastic bowl and the end of a rolling pin.

4 Place your smashed aromatics in the sterilised jar or bottle.

5 Heat your oil of choice over a low heat in the saucepan until you begin to see it simmer.

6 Add your oil to the jar (a funnel is useful here, if you have one), seal, then leave it to infuse.

7 After 2 hours, strain the herbs or other flavourings out of your jar into the bottle through the sieve and – ta-da! – you're good to go.

8 Make sure to place your bottle in a dark cool spot out of the sunlight. Use it up within 2 months.

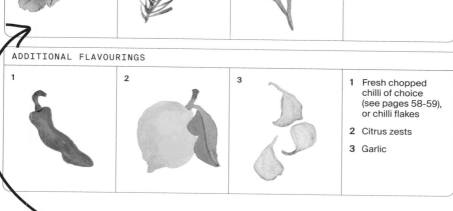

HERB IDEAS

1	2	3
5	7	8

1 Basil
2 Bay leaf
3 Chives
4 Dill
5 Mint
6 Oregano
7 Rosemary
8 Sage
9 Tarragon
10 Thyme

ADDITIONAL FLAVOURINGS

1	2	3

1 Fresh chopped chilli of choice (see pages 58-59), or chilli flakes

2 Citrus zests

3 Garlic

REMOVING ALL THE WATER PREVENTS BACTERIA FROM GROWING

USING A DARK BOTTLE WILL PREVENT OXIDATION + KEEP YOUR OIL FRESHER

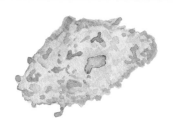

SALT

Salt is a controversial condiment. As you know (see page 25), I like to ask people what their top three condiments are, and I ask myself frequently, too. Though my second and third choices change daily (Dijon mustard will always be #1), if I mention salt, arguments tend to begin. As with butter, there is salt the ingredient, then there is salt the condiment. **A finishing salt is a condiment**, the grand finale of a dish, the last word. It can be crunchy, flaky, colourful and even have an added flavour.

When you sprinkle sea salt flakes over basic buttered pasta, you're levelling up the dish and adding a condiment. Smoked salt scattered over a lovely seared piece of fish? Condiment. A pinch of cinnamon-vanilla salt to finish off a vanilla sponge cake? Condiment. A dusting of tajin on a fruit salad? Condiment.

Please don't salt your food before tasting it. Don't get me wrong, I **LOVE** salt*. I am known to keep both soy sauce packets and sea salt flakes in my bag in case of emergencies. However, salt must be used wisely, not just for the sake of it. Take a first bite, see what's missing: is it actually salt? Is it texture? Is it acidity? This will depend on your flavour preferences. I usually miss acidity in a dish, so I reach for a dollop of mustard or a squeeze of lemon juice. However, if I do find salt is that missing puzzle piece, I'll reach into my bag for my emergency flaky rations.

Salt comes in many shapes and sizes. The odds are, if you visit a new country, you'll find a different salt on the table to the type you have at home. Don't dismiss this, look into it! I have learned fascinating cultural information based on salt itself: its use, pungency, purpose, makers and production process.

Regardless of its regional name, shape, colour and taste, all salt is made from the same mineral: NaCl, or sodium chloride. It's the most glorious little compound, which not only enhances flavour and promotes aroma, but also acts as a preservative by curing or fermenting.

All salt originates from a body of water. As time progresses and millions of years pass, some bodies of water (unsurprisingly) dry up, their only remains being salt. In the present day, salt can be divided into two sources: water (ocean, sea, lake, river) and rock salt mines.

Like that of wine, the *terroir* of a salt will determine its flavour. This simply means that, depending on its environment (think: geography, geology, climate) as well as its method of harvest, **all salts will taste slightly distinct from each other**. Added minerals and compounds will affect their taste, colour and more. A salt's texture also changes its flavour; remember how even chewing in different ways can affect the way you perceive taste (see page 20)? A coarse salt will leave a different impression on your tongue – and crunch in between your teeth – than a finer salt that will dissolve subtly in your mouth. Each has an individually beautiful structure that should determine its usage, whether you cook with it or use it as a finishing salt.

Seasoning is everything. Salt can and should be used in all forms of cooking, but judiciously. It is an angelic mechanism to draw out and amplify flavour and to counterbalance blander foods. Bland isn't bad, it's simply neutral and needs a little extra help from our salty friends: think of scrumptious toasty bread, steaming fluffy white rice, or pasta dancing in a pan at a rolling boil.

Worried about oversalting? Undersalting? Salinity depends on the exact salt you choose as well as the amount you're using, so just add it little by little, tasting as you go, until you're perfectly content.

History of salt

The range of salt's story is vast and has been the subject of many books (see page 181). Ancient Egyptians were the first to recognise, in around 2,000 BCE, that sodium drew moisture not only out of food but also out of humans. Egyptian mummies were commonly packed in salt to ensure their preservation and then shipped down the Nile. These corpses were literally taxed as salted meat! Ancient Romans also believed salt had curing properties, in many senses: it could cure meat as well as ailments. While some of us may know that the word salary stems from the Latin word for salt, *sal,* did you know that the Latin term for wellbeing was *salus*? Salt was a common medicine for all afflictions, from respiratory to skin to digestive. Due to its all-important nature and numerous uses, *sal* is the root of many words. Even the term soldier comes from *sal-dare*, or 'to give salt', as these men were paid in salt.

Though it has been highly venerated and used in numerous ways throughout millennia, let's just focus on salt the condiment, rather than salt the ingredient.

SALTY HUMAN (TAXABLE CARGO) COMING THROUGH

* I really do not **LOVE** pepper. I am a super taster, so there are certain flavours that overwhelm my palate and unfortunately pepper is among them. One taste of pepper and I can't taste anything else for the following minutes. Salt and pepper are the perfect pair and used in most recipes, including those in this book; however, if you're ever eating at my house, you will probably not find pepper in any dish.

Different types of salt

Table salt

- A refined salt that comes from the sea, or is mined from underground salt deposits
- Fine-grained
- Added iodine and anti-caking agents make it the only non-shelf-stable salt out there; any other salt is good forever
- It has a sharper flavour (a little goes a long way!)

Mined salt

- All mined salt is harvested from ancient dried-up bodies of water. Many types come in surprising colours and have especially distinct flavours, due to minerals surrounding them in the ground

1 HIMALAYAN PINK SALT

This all comes from the same mine in Pakistan in the Khewra mountain range (a few hundred miles from the Himalayas). The colour comes from different minerals, such as iron.

2 PERSIAN BLUE DIAMOND SALT

Sourced from a single ancient salt lake in Iran. The blue colour comes from a mineral called sylvinite and the structure of the salt further refracts blue light.

3 KALA NAMAK

A Himalayan salt that has been sealed in a ceramic jar with bark, herbs, seeds and charcoal, burned in a furnace for a day, then further aged. It has a deep maroon-brownish hue and smells of egg from its high sulphur content, a facet which means it's used in many vegan recipes.

4 KOSHER SALT

Coarse, additive-free salt that dissolves quickly and is frequently used in cooking. Kosher meat must have the blood removed before eating, so this salt is used to draw it out.

Sea salt

- If sea salt has an interesting flaky texture, it's a finishing salt. If it's fine-grained, cook with it!
- As it's made from evaporated sea water from different *terroirs*, all have slightly different flavours and textures
- It dissolves on the tongue
- Standard supermarket sea salt is produced by man-made evaporation
- More luxurious sea salts are naturally evaporated in pans and harvested by hand

5 FLEUR DE SEL

White salt harvested from the surface of the water by hand with wooden rakes, as if it were luscious cream on top of milk.

6 GREY SALT

Also known as sel gris, this salt is harvested from the bottom of the same pans used for fleur de sel. It is coarse and grey in colour because of the compounds and minerals found below. It is also called 'Celtic salt' after the original Celtic hand-harvesting method.

7 MALDON

A coarse, irregular flaky salt.

8 HALEN MÔN

Delicate, crystal-clear, flaky salt hand-picked in Anglesey, Wales.

9 HAWAIIAN BLACK SALT

Naturally evaporated sea salt blended with coconut shell-activated charcoal.

10 HAWAIIAN RED SALT

Naturally evaporated sea salt blended with alaea – a volcanic clay rich in iron – which gives a brick-red colour.

11 CYPRUS BLACK LAVA SALT

As with Hawaiian black salt, this is mixed with activated charcoal, but this time the salt is from the Mediterranean Sea.

12 FIRE SALT

As the name suggests, this comes from brine that is heated over fire to expose the salt crystals. This can be done quickly or slowly, changing the composition of the crystals (slower = smaller, faster = chunkier).

13 SHIO SALT

This Japanese salt comes from a very slowly boiled brine, which results in delicate tiny crystals.

14 IBURI JIO

A Japanese fire salt that is roasted over a cherry-wood fire to complete the drying process and give a smoked flavour.

15 BALENI SALT

Created by a process involving both solar and fire evaporation! Obtained from a swamp formed by a mineral spring in South Africa, this salt is harvested and boiled by the women of the Tsonga tribe and seen as a sacred salt. Brine is mixed with clean sand, hand-filtered through a frame made of leaves and branches, then eventually boiled over metal pans. Once salt crystals appear, the women create salt cones and leave them to dry in the sun.

5

10

MY FAVOURITE

How to make flavoured salt

As with all condiments, there are no rules here: mix and match flavours as you please. And there's no need to buy a new fancy variety, just play around with whatever salt you have sitting in your kitchen.

Salt can be used in brines, dressings, batters, doughs, butter, as a finishing crunchy topper... *as a condiment*. It's been years since I began sprinkling salt on top of fruit shakes, smoothies, freshly baked cookies or honey, and I've never stopped. The contrast between their sweet taste and a crunchy grain of salt is a simple but powerful mouthfeel and gives a burst of flavour.

- Pick your salt of choice, if you don't have any in the kitchen: I gravitate towards fleur de sel or Maldon salt for flavoured blends.

- Choose the ingredients you'd like to add. If they include fresh herbs or citrus zests, make sure to dry these out on a baking tray in a low temperature oven (preheated to 100°C) before combining them with the salt. Any spice or dried herb can be used as is.

- Combine your herbs, spices or zests with the salt. I prefer a prominent salt flavour, so I use a 2:1 salt-to-flavouring ratio. You can always add more or less, as you prefer.

- All that's left to do is jar up and enjoy! Flavoured salt makes a great gift and the flavourings can be tailored to different seasons of the year, such as adding warming spices for autumn (see opposite).

SOME OF MY FAVOURITE FLAVOURED SALT COMBOS

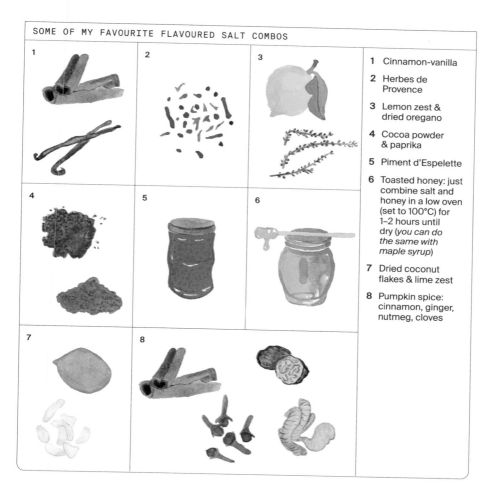

1 Cinnamon-vanilla

2 Herbes de Provence

3 Lemon zest & dried oregano

4 Cocoa powder & paprika

5 Piment d'Espelette

6 Toasted honey: just combine salt and honey in a low oven (set to 100°C) for 1–2 hours until dry (*you can do the same with maple syrup*)

7 Dried coconut flakes & lime zest

8 Pumpkin spice: cinnamon, ginger, nutmeg, cloves

Everything bagel seasoning

And as a final favourite, I like mixing a **makeshift everything bagel seasoning** using ingredients from the traditional bagel blend as well as elements from Japanese furikake.

Just combine toasted black and white sesame seeds, poppy seeds, garlic and onion flakes and nori (*and if you're feeling extra-funky, toss in some bonito flakes, shichimi togarishi and a pinch of sugar, too*)

DIPS

SAVOURY
+ SWEET

SAVOURY DIPS

YOUR KEY TO
MISH-MASH DINNERS

Dips are controversial 'condiments'. What exactly makes them a condiment? Their usage. If you're dipping a crudité into something that you can also use it as a spread, it's a condiment in my book. Hummus? It depends. When used as a dip, hummus is a condiment. Served as a whole dish? Not a condiment.

These dips are **fleeting, tasty memories** and don't keep as long as other jarred condiments. All the recipes in the next few pages, both savoury and sweet, are quick to make with little-to-no preparation, as all you need to do is mix all the ingredients and *voilà*!

My mother's Greek heritage has strongly influenced my dippage game: the Mediterranean world really understands a spread-and-dip. I believe that any *apéro* should begin with a minimum of a trio of dips, to be mixed and matched depending on the condiment vessel of choice (*turn the page for a veritable cornucopia of ideas for those*). A crudité platter allows guests to explore different condiments, all while staying true to those flavours to which their palates are more geared. Every person can thus create a mish-mash, or stick to their favourite flavour combo, all while sharing the same experience.

I don't know if I'll ever love any dish more than a crudité platter. Make it for yourself, put it together for friends, it's perfect either way. There are innumerable combinations of vegetables and dips and it's now one of my (*many*) condiment missions to try every single possible permutation.

Storing fresh dips

If not eaten in one sitting, though leftovers are a rare event, all the savoury dips on the following pages will need to be eaten within two or three days and stored in the fridge, since they use fresh ingredients. (Return them to room temperature to serve, for the best flavours)

Crudité platters

Apart from condiments, the key to a great crudité platter is how you cut the vegetables. You want a variety of shapes and sizes, not only to intrigue the eye, but also to create different condiment matches. For ease of condiment transport, as well as for visual purposes, I also always favour veggies with a stem.

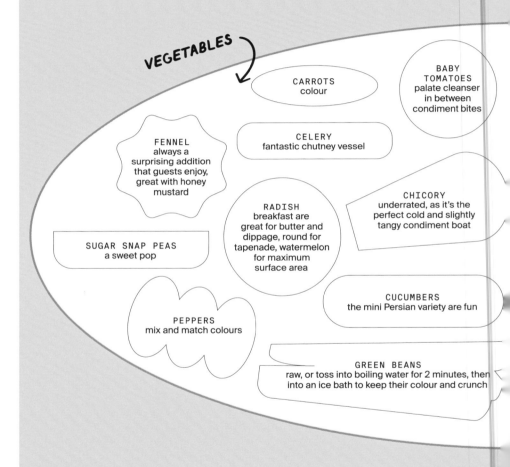

VEGETABLES

CARROTS
colour

BABY TOMATOES
palate cleanser in between condiment bites

FENNEL
always a surprising addition that guests enjoy, great with honey mustard

CELERY
fantastic chutney vessel

CHICORY
underrated, as it's the perfect cold and slightly tangy condiment boat

RADISH
breakfast are great for butter and dippage, round for tapenade, watermelon for maximum surface area

SUGAR SNAP PEAS
a sweet pop

CUCUMBERS
the mini Persian variety are fun

PEPPERS
mix and match colours

GREEN BEANS
raw, or toss into boiling water for 2 minutes, then into an ice bath to keep their colour and crunch

Place different-coloured vegetables next to each other. For example, I wouldn't place celery next to cucumber, or red peppers next to tomatoes. However, if you choose to go with a single colour – say green – for the entire platter, then lean into it! Serve all your green veg with Simple herby feta, Green tapenade (see pages 164 and 165), green olives, cornichons and so on.

In terms of texture, mix it up! Hummus has quite a distinct texture from, say, honey Dijon or chutney. Play around with combinations you enjoy: see if you like a certain vegetable with a specific condiment because of mouthfeel, taste, aroma or colour.

REMEMBER COLOUR
+ TEXTURE!
THE EYES FEAST
BEFORE THE
STOMACH

COLD AND COOL DIPS
caesar, ranch, tzatziki,
melitzanosalata, hummus, tapenade
(see pages 142, 144, 162,
163, 164 and 165)

SWEET
fruit-heavy chutney,
jam (*Tomato-vanilla-
basil*, see page 87,
is always fun)

SPICE
chilli crisp, spicy plum
chutney, Candied jalapeño bites,
kimchi (*great inside chicory leaf boats*),
homemade hot sauce to mix
into any of them (see pages 105, 60,
124 and 66)

ACID
any pickle or ferment,
Quick pickled red onions
(see pages 112–135)

SALT
don't forget about flavoured
salts (see page 154)! These are a
great addition not only for breakfast
radishes and butter, but also
for watery veg

CONDIMENTS

Lastly, I'll leave you with this thought. It is **SO** satisfying to build your crudité platter using all homemade condiments (make little name cards for them, gauge what your guests like best). It helps you to work out how you might tweak your recipes next time, as most of my feedback comes from serving condiments to my friends and seeing how the majority responds to each. Everyone will have a different combo of choice. For example, I love:

- black tapenade & radishes
- green tapenade & chicory
- carrots & honey Dijon
- red peppers & pickle
- cucumber & flavoured salts
- green beans & hummus & Dijon

161

Tzatziki

It really is impossible to pick a favourite dip, because the combinations are endless, but tzatziki is high up on my list. It's fresh, bright and sour so it pairs wonderfully with almost everything. Tzatziki and roast grilled fish? With lamb? Or crisp cold vegetables? Piping hot pitta? I still haven't found anything it doesn't enhance. It marries well with all temperatures and textures and gives that extra oomph without overpowering your vessel of choice.

My mum doesn't just like dill, she **LOVES** dill and puts it in almost everything. I grew up eating a very dill-heavy tzatziki because of her, so, to me, this flavour is one of pure comfort.

WHAT YOU NEED

½ cucumber, deseeded
pinch of salt
450g full-fat Greek yogurt
1 tbsp wine vinegar (*ideally red but white also works*)
bunch of dill (*yes, it's a lot*), chopped

1 tbsp chopped mint leaves
finely grated zest and juice of 1 lemon
good olive oil
2 bowls
colander

WHAT TO DO

1   Grate the cucumber and place in one of the bowls.

2   Add the pinch of salt to the cucumber, massage throughout and leave to drain in the colander while you get on with prepping the remainder of the ingredients.

3   Put your yogurt in the other bowl with the vinegar, dill, mint, lemon zest and juice.

4   Squeeze out any remaining liquid from the cucumber and add it to the yogurt bowl. Stir gently to amalgamate.

5   Serve topped with a drizzle of olive oil.

PAIRING IDEAS

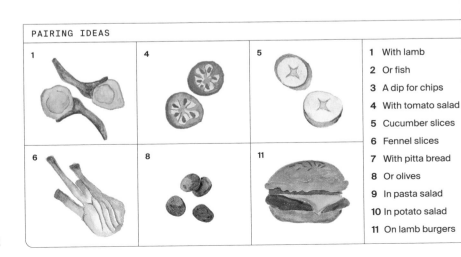

1   With lamb
2   Or fish
3   A dip for chips
4   With tomato salad
5   Cucumber slices
6   Fennel slices
7   With pitta bread
8   Or olives
9   In pasta salad
10 In potato salad
11 On lamb burgers

Melitzanosalata

Literally just aubergine – *melitzana* – and salad – *salata* – in Greek. The Greek version doesn't contain tahini, which gives a creamy texture and nutty flavour to the more common Middle Eastern babaganoush. Instead, this is a chunky, citrusy, vegetable-forward dish.

WHAT YOU NEED

2 tbsp good olive oil, plus
    more for the vegetables
    and to serve
salt
2 aubergines
1 pepper

1 garlic clove
finely grated zest and
    juice of 2 lemons
1–2 tbsp chopped parsley leaves
colander
bowl

WHAT TO DO

1. Drizzle olive oil and salt on the aubergines and pepper.

2. Roast the aubergines and pepper – ideally directly over a flame on a gas hob – for 10–15 minutes, or until charred and soft. (Using the grill in the oven will also work, but will take closer to 30 minutes.) Either way, you'll want to have the extractor fan going.

3. Once soft, scoop out the insides of the charred aubergines, chop them up and place in the colander to drain out some of the juices.

4. Remove the seeds from the pepper (no need to peel), chop and transfer to the same colander.

5. After 10–15 minutes, once both have cooled down, transfer to the bowl. More liquid than you'd expect will have come out.

6. Grate in the garlic clove and pour in the juice of both lemons, salt to taste and add the 2 tbsp olive oil. Mix well.

7. Finish it off with the chopped parsley, lemon zest and salt to taste and an extra drizzle of good olive oil.

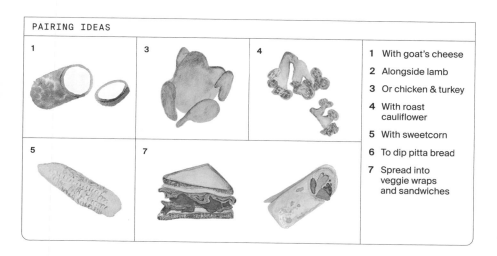

PAIRING IDEAS

1. With goat's cheese
2. Alongside lamb
3. Or chicken & turkey
4. With roast cauliflower
5. With sweetcorn
6. To dip pitta bread
7. Spread into veggie wraps and sandwiches

Fava-style hummus

I can already see the look on many of your faces when reading this recipe... *'Claire! Where is the tahini?'* In my recipe, it's simply not there. It's not a printing error, I can assure you. My Greek family focuses on lemon and garlic when making their hummus. There is another dip in Greece called fava made with yellow split peas. In my family, we make a fava dip with chickpeas instead, or should that be a hummus in the same style as fava? My flavour profile is more drawn to acidity – hence the lemon juice – than to silky, creamy or fatty. If you are more into the latter, more traditional Middle Eastern hummus, feel free to stir 1 tbsp of tahini into the finished dish.

400g can of chickpeas
1–2 garlic cloves
3 tbsp good olive oil
juice of 2 lemons (*trust me*)
¼ tsp ground cumin
¼ tsp salt
blender

Drain the chickpeas.

Put the chickpeas in the blender with the garlic, 2 tbsp of the olive oil, the juice of 1½ lemons, the cumin and salt.

Blend until smooth. Check the consistency and add 1 tbsp of water at a time if the hummus is too thick.

Serve topped with the remaining 1 tbsp of olive oil and lemon juice.

Simple herby feta

This is an untraditional Greek dip with traditional Greek flavours. Forgive me ancestors, it's **TOO** easy and **TOO** delicious to omit from the book.

Don't have any dried oregano or dill? Don't worry! Replace them with another dried herb or herb blend of your choice: try herbes de Provence, parsley or basil.

200–225g block of feta cheese
1 tsp dried oregano
1 tsp dried dill
3 tbsp good olive oil, plus more to serve
pinch of chilli flakes (optional)
finely grated zest and juice of 1 lemon,
to taste
blender (optional)

Mix the feta, herbs, oil and chilli, if using, by blending or simply smooshing.

Drizzle with more oil and a squeeze of lemon juice, to taste, then grate over a little zest, again using as much as you like.

PAIRING IDEAS	
	1 With root vegetables (*raw or cooked*)
	2 Or peppers
	3 With pitta bread
	4 To dip tortilla chips
	5 With dark leafy greens (*such as kale or spinach*)

PAIRING IDEAS	
	1 With fresh fruit (*try grapes & stone fruit*)
	2 With eggs
	3 Spread on pitta bread
	4 Or seeded bread
	5 On bagels with smoked salmon
	6 With cucumber
	7 Or radishes
	8 Or beetroot

Black tapenade

Not Greek, but French. Though I like to use Kalamata olives in it. This may shock you, but black tapenade contains anchovies and may even be your gateway dip to loving that delectable 'bacon of the sea'.

Both these tapenades are lovely chopped rather than blended, so give that a go if you ever have the time and inclination.

290g can of pitted black olives
(165g drained weight)
1 tbsp capers in brine
1 tsp caper brine
1–2 tbsp chopped parsley leaves
1 tsp anchovy paste, or 2–3 anchovies
2 garlic cloves (*for the brave, reduce
to 1 if you're not a fan*)
2 tbsp good olive oil, plus more if needed
(*if your mixture is too thick*)
1 tbsp lemon juice
blender, or knife

Drain the olives and reserve 1 tbsp of the brine.

If using a blender, put the olives and the 1 tbsp of their brine in the blender jug and add the capers and their brine, the parsley, anchovy paste or anchovies, garlic, olive oil and lemon juice. Then blend.

If chopping by hand, chop the solid ingredients, then mix in the liquids. It's seriously so easy. If it is too thick, add a little more olive oil gradually until the consistency is as you like it.

Green tapenade

To keep the colour of this intact, I don't include any anchovies. It's my version of green goddess dip with some extra personality. Don't have all these herbs? Don't worry! Add whatever you have to hand, even if they're not listed here. Play around with it, you can't go wrong.

290g can of pitted green olives
(165g drained weight)
1 tbsp olive brine
1 tbsp capers
1 tsp caper brine
1 garlic clove
2–4 tbsp chopped parsley leaves
2–3 tbsp chopped basil leaves
1–2 tbsp chopped dill
1 tbsp chopped chives
finely grated zest and juice of 1 lemon
2 tbsp good olive oil
blender, or knife

Just blend, or chop away, as in the recipe left.

WHEN I AM LOOKING TO DEEPEN A DISH, I OPT FOR BLACK TAPENADE, BUT WHEN I WANT TO BRIGHTEN ONE, I GO FOR GREEN

PAIRING IDEAS	
2	1 With tomato-based dishes
	2 Or goat's cheese
	3 Stirred into dark leafy greens
6	4 On pissaladière
	5 In a tarte Tatin
	6 Or a quiche

PAIRING IDEAS	
1	1 With soft fresh cheese such as ricotta
	2 With white fish
	3 As a dip with endive
3	4 One of my favourites on a crudité platter
	5 With whole boiled globe artichokes
5	6 On grilled courgettes

SWEET DIPS

My dear sweet-toothed readers, I didn't forget about you in this chapter. While the recipes in the pages that follow can be used as spreads, I have also dipped many fun snacks in them and obtained maximal flavour pleasure. These sweet dips are the perfect option for when you come home and need a sweet treat, but have nothing in your kitchen cupboards or even in the fridge. I often find myself tipping random cereal, nuts, seeds and spices into yogurt and calling it my 'dessert dip' at the end of a chaotic day.

Whether you use the recipes in these pages, or boil some frozen berries and make a coulis, prep some chia seed pudding, or mix yogurt with miscellaneous pantry items, sweet dips will have your back.

In terms of dippage, feel free to **use your imagination**, as well as random ingredients lying around your home: carrots, crisps, popcorn, celery, breadsticks, frozen banana slices, apple slices... Fun snicky-snack platters don't need to be savoury. I personally love sprinkling carrot sticks with cinnamon vanilla salt and dipping them in a mixture of yogurt, cinnamon, coconut flakes and rice pops; sometimes I even add a dollop of jam to **amp it up**!

How to make nutty butter

What you need to remember is, regardless of your nut or seed of preference, you can *always* make a scrumptious butter with it. As long as you have a blender, you're good to go, so feel free to mix types of nuts, seeds and spices.

WHAT YOU NEED

250–275g unsweetened raw nuts or seeds of choice
(*almonds, cashews, peanuts, pistachios, pumpkin seeds, sunflower seeds, you get the point!*)
baking tray
blender or food processor
spatula (*so needed to scrape down the nutty mess*)

sterilised jar (see page 74)
Optional add-ins
salt
miso (see page 130 for homemade)
vanilla extract
ground cinnamon
cocoa powder
ground ginger
chilli powder
desiccated coconut

WHAT TO DO

1 Preheat the oven to 180°C. Roast the nuts on the baking tray for around 10 minutes. (*Trust your instinct: if you think they're getting too dark, pull them out earlier.*)

2 Tip the toasty nuts into the blender or food processor and begin to blend. Go slowly, blend for a few seconds, stop, scrape down the sides with the spatula and start again. If you blend too fast, the nut butter will overheat and turn into a hot sticky clump (*and your blender will be very unhappy*). Each nut will take a different amount of time to blend, but it shouldn't be more than 5 minutes in total.

3 Once your nut butter has come together, it's time for your add-ins. Place any of these you want in the blender or food processor.

4 Give your combination of dreams a last whizz, then jar up!

5 Store the nutty butter in the fridge; it should last you at least a few months, if not longer.

PAIRING IDEAS

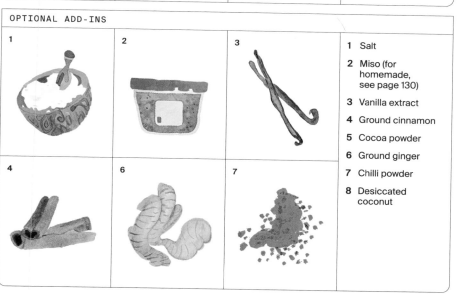

1   **1** In PB&Js (see page 170)

2 In dressing for salad or noodles

3 As a crudité dip

4 In yogurt parfaits

5 With pancakes

6 Or frozen banana slices

7 As part of an apple nacho platter with My spiced & boozy cajeta (see page 173)

OPTIONAL ADD-INS

1 Salt

2 Miso (for homemade, see page 130)

3 Vanilla extract

4 Ground cinnamon

5 Cocoa powder

6 Ground ginger

7 Chilli powder

8 Desiccated coconut

An illustrated guide to a grown-up PB&J

Nut butters and jelly are a match made in condiment heaven. This is your illustrated and ultimately versatile guide to layering their flavours and textures.

THE BUTTER LAYER

PEANUT   **ALMOND**

THE JAM OR JELLY LAYER

GRAPE   **BLUEBERRY**   **FIG**

THE SPICE LAYER

GROUND CINNAMON   **PAPRIKA**

THE CRUNCH

SALT   **CACAO NIBS**

THE FRUIT

BANANA   **FIG**   **BLUEBERRY**

I'M PERSONALLY A GRAPE-JELLY-AND-CRUNCHY-PEANUT-BUTTER-WITH-EXTRA-SEA-SALT-FLAKES-AND-A-SPRINKLE-OF-CINNAMON-ON-TOP KIND OF GIRL

PISTACHIO

HAZELNUT

CHESTNUT

STRAWBERRY

APRICOT

QUINCE

PEAR

GROUND CARDAMOM

GROUND CUMIN

CHILLI FLAKES

COCONUT FLAKES

DRIED FRUIT

TOASTED SESAME

HEMP SEEDS

GRAPES

RASPBERRY

STRAWBERRY

CHERRY

My chestnut spread

Ah, the famed French *crème de marrons*. No need to fly to France to taste this absolute *délice*, all you need is to get your hands on some chestnuts! It's easier than you think to make.

My recipe is a bit different, as I like to add a pinch of instant coffee to bring out the deep roasty-toasty flavours. If you don't have any to hand, don't worry! You'll just be making it more authentically.

WHAT YOU NEED

240ml water
½ tsp instant coffee
65g caster sugar
200g cooked chestnuts
2 tsp vanilla extract
big pinch of salt
saucepan
food processor or hand blender
sterilised jars (see page 74)

WHAT TO DO

1   Combine your measured water, instant coffee and sugar in the saucepan and simmer until both are fully dissolved. Turn off the heat.

2   Place your chestnuts in the food processor or the tall vessel of a hand blender and purée.

3   Once the sugar mixture has cooled off, pour it into the food processor or blender vessel with the chestnuts and blend again until all are incorporated (make sure not to blend when the liquid is hot, as that can be dangerous).

4   Return the chestnut mixture to the saucepan and add the vanilla and salt.

5   Set the saucepan over a low heat and begin to slowly mix, to combine all the elements.

6   Continue to mix for around 10 minutes until you've got a thick paste, then turn off the heat.

7   Pot the spread into the jars and enjoy! Once opened, store in the fridge, where it will keep for a few months.

PAIRING IDEAS

1

2

3

1   With fresh cheese
2   Or yogurt
3   In crêpes (see page 174)
4   Over waffles & toast

My spiced & boozy cajeta

You will have heard of dulce de leche. An easy way to make it is by boiling a jar of condensed milk and *voilà*, a warm, teddy bear-brown caramel which falls in thick ribbons. The milk means it's silkier and has a richer texture than regular caramel. *Cajeta* is the Mexican version, a speciality of Celaya in the state of Guanajuato, made from goat's milk. Since goat's milk is tangier than cow's milk, I find this version less cloyingly sweet and with a more interesting aftertaste. You do not need to add the cinnamon or rum. I find they elevate the flavour, but these things are personal.

WHAT YOU NEED

1 litre goat's milk
200g granulated sugar
pinch of salt
1 cinnamon stick (optional)
½ tsp bicarbonate of soda
1 tsp vanilla extract
1–2 tbsp spiced rum (optional)
saucepan
sterilised jar (see page 74)

WHAT TO DO

1   Place your milk, sugar, salt and cinnamon stick, if using, in the saucepan. Make sure your pan has some room at the top as this is going to boil and poof up a bit! You don't want a sticky mess. Set over a medium-low heat and stir continuously.

2   Dissolve the bicarbonate of soda in a cup in around 1 tsp of water.

3   Once your milk starts turning from white to light toasty brown, remove from the heat and add the bicarb mixture. It will go crazy and froth up; this is normal, just stir-stir-stir to bring it down.

4   Once the mixture has calmed down a bit, return it to the heat and continue to stir for another good 30–45 minutes until golden, caramel-like ribbons form under your spoon.

5   Texture is a personal preference, but if you intend this for a cake or cookie filling, you may want it a bit thicker. I prefer mine thinner and silkier, to add to drinks or drizzle over fruit.

6   Once you're happy with your *cajeta*, turn off the heat and remove the cinnamon stick, if you used it. Add the vanilla extract and rum, if using, and stir once more.

7   Spoon into the sterilised jar and keep it in the fridge.

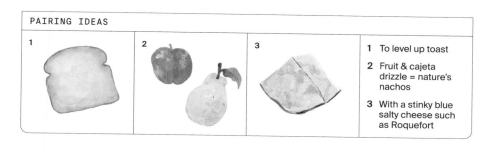

PAIRING IDEAS

1   To level up toast

2   Fruit & cajeta drizzle = nature's nachos

3   With a stinky blue salty cheese such as Roquefort

Crêpes

My biggest claim to fame is being featured on Nicola Lamb's iconic *Kitchen Projects* newsletter for my crêpe recipe. Never in my life did I think my recipe was unique, but it turns out that using beer as a major ingredient isn't too common. Regardless, this works every time. Beware, if you're making these for friends, that they'll ask you to make more, so you may as well whip up a giant batch. Crêpes are basically thin discs of air, so you **COULD** realistically eat five hundred in a single sitting. (Don't panic; this recipe makes more like twenty.) If you can't eat all of them, they can be refrigerated and enjoyed for up to a week, or frozen for later.

There are so many fun combinations when it comes to crêpes. This is a sweet crêpe recipe, so please don't add cheese or ham to it, I can't disrespect my ancestors like that. I did not include a galette recipe in the book because a *galette complète* (with ham, eggs and cheese) is perfect on its own and needs no condiments (*never thought you'd hear me say that, right?*)

WHAT YOU NEED

250g plain flour, plus more
if needed
240ml milk, plus more
if needed
240ml beer *(I tend to opt*
for lager here, but it really
doesn't matter)
3 eggs, lightly beaten

1 tsp vanilla extract
1 hefty tbsp or 15g melted butter,
or neutral oil, plus more to cook
pinch of salt
pinch of sugar
bowl
whisk
frying pan

WHAT TO DO

For the batter

1 Put the flour in the bowl and make a well in the centre.

2 Add the milk slowly while whisking, making sure there are no lumps.

3 Pour in the beer, eggs and vanilla extract, still whisking all the time.

4 Now add the melted butter or oil to the bowl and whisk.

5 Finally add your salt and sugar, whisk the batter again, cover and pop in the fridge.

6 At this stage, the batter should run freely from a spoon, but coat it fully, and should have quite a liquid consistency similar to kefir or drinking yogurt. If it's too thick, add more milk 1 tbsp at a time; if it is too thin, add 1 tbsp of flour at a time.

7 Rest the batter in the fridge for at least 2 hours; the longer it's left, the tangier and lighter each crêpe will be. Expect the batter to thicken. (You can technically use this batter right away, but it is better after a rest.)

To cook the crêpes, a little batter goes a long way

8   Heat a pan over a medium heat, add a knob of butter and sacrifice your first crêpe: like pancakes, the first will be a bit off because it will soak up all the butter (*don't worry, chef's treat*).

9   It's time to get started on the perfect crêpes! Plop some batter (about 35g) into the pan and let's do this again. A little batter goes a long way, don't underestimate the spread of these skinny legends.

10 Cook for 1 minute, then flip and cook for another 30–60 seconds. Is it ready? Just look at the colour! It's a matter of preference.

11 **Repeat!**

12 Finally, it's time to feast. Serve up with your favourite condiments.

FOR CRÊPES

FAVOURITE CONDIMENTS

1   Chestnut spread (for homemade, see page 172)

2   Lemon and sugar

3   Pear & chocolate (*use fresh pears and dark chocolate sauce, or even try with Pear & lemongrass jam, see page 86*)

4   Any jam really (see pages 82–87)

5   Maple syrup, soy and cinnamon salt (*American-French mish-mash crêpe?*) I always add soy to my maple syrup

ODDS + ENDS

My fondest desire is that you attempt some of my recipes and end up changing them, to suit yourself. How beautiful is it that we all have varied flavour predilections based on our unique experiences and palates? All I wish is for you to fully explore yourself and your own flavour preferences. If you take anything from this book, I hope it is that you learned more about **what flavour profiles and combinations you're drawn to**.

If you need a final reason to dive deep into condiments, here it is: they highlight **sustainable** practices. Yes, you can reuse leftover jars for varying reasons (see overleaf) or recycle them, but I'm touching on avoiding food waste here. Any leftover herbs can be chucked into a dressing, a dip or a salad. And yes, I mentioned earlier that unripe fruit is better suited for jam because of its higher pectin levels, but that doesn't mean it's **NEEDED**. Rather than throwing mushy bruised fruit away, make it into a coulis, a jam, chutney or cake. Food should never be thrown away, so think how you can *condiment* it – and let's claim that word as a verb – next time you are about to pop open the rubbish bin.

I love using the near-empty jars themselves to present these new, repurposed condiments. Whether it's for guests and you're serving a cocktail in a cute glass, dressing a salad at the table, or placing a dip in the middle of a crudité platter, jars add some fun to the tablescape. When it's just me, I love the **magic** involved in placing my leftovers in jars with the delicious last scraps of a condiment and completely changing their flavour (see opposite).

Nearly leftover jars?

Do you have any jars in your fridge or cupboard you can't seem to get rid of? The ones you shove to the back of the shelf and just hope will somehow disappear? Here are a few ways to use these nearly-empty jars. Just add some extra ingredients to said jar, shake and enjoy washing up one less plate or bowl!

1 JAM, HONEY OR JELLY

Use in cocktails, salad dressings, yogurt and chia puddings, or add wine to create a glaze or marinade for meat and veggies

2 CHUTNEY

Good in salad dressings and dolloped alongside most salads, too

3 MAYO

Add to salads, Caesar dressing or Bright ranch (see pages 142 and 144)

4 MUSTARD, CHILLI CRISP OR JAM

Use in marinades, scrambled eggs, salad dressings, savoury leftovers, salads or dips

5 KETCHUP

Use in dips, or add to sauces and glazes (*it is the perfect mother sauce*)

6 PICKLE BRINE

Great in marinades, salad dressings and salads, or toss some favourite fruit or veggies into the brine and make a quick pickle (see page 117)

7 PEANUT BUTTER

Add to a delicious marinade with miso, ponzu or soy sauce (for homemade versions see pages 130 and 134), or use in salad dressings, yogurt, chia puddings, smoothies and shakes

How to reuse jars

As storage for spices,
seeds or seasoning

For an unique candle vessel

As Tupperware:
make leftovers chic

As a cocktail shaker:
great when the jar contains
the ends of a jam or jelly

For a small planter to grow
and sprout seeds

As a flower vase

For gift giving: granola, jams, flavoured oils
(see pages 84 and 146)

As a decoration: a snow globe,
or a tea light holder

To nurture a sourdough starter

To serve dips
at a dinner party

As a cutlery holder
on a table

As a piggy bank

Or a pen holder

For a salad dressing mixing vessel, especially when
the jar contained mustard, mayo or chutney

Further reading

↳ (+ *LISTENING*)

BOOKS

13 Foods That Shape Our World, Alex Renton

Cooking Apicius: Roman Recipes for Today, Sally Grainger

On Va Déguster: La France, François-Régis Gaudry & Ses Amis

Jam Bake, Camilla Wynne

Fermenter Presque Tout avec Presque Rien, Juliette Patissier

A Cook's Tour: Global Adventures in Extreme Cuisine, Anthony Bourdain

Hot Sauce Nation: America's Burning Obsession, Denver Nicks

The Edible Book Series, The University of Chicago Press

Gastrophysics: The New Science of Eating, Charles Spence

Scoff: A History of Food and Class in Britain, Pen Vogler

A Natural History of the Senses, Diane Ackerman

The Noma Guide to Fermentation, René Redzepi and David Zilber

Asian Pickles: Sweet, Sour, Salty, Cured, and Fermented Preserves, Karen Solomon

Of Cabbages and Kimchi, James Read

Salt Fat Acid Heat, Samin Nosrat

Salt: A World History, Mark Kurlansky

In Search of Lost Time, Marcel Proust

Nicola Lamb Kitchen Projects Substack

PODCASTS

Simon Majumdar Eat My Globe

Gastropod: Food with a Side of Science & History

Condiments & cultures

I want to celebrate all condiments, not just those I grew up with from France, Greece or America, so I have included recipes for quick and easy condiments from around the world in this book. I have done my best to educate myself, not just on flavour, but also on cultures other than my own. I am very lucky to have a community of friends and food professionals from around the world who have helped me in this effort. My intention is to respect these different cultures and their culinary traditions. We can all learn from each other, my way in is just through my tastebuds, as well as by means of written and oral histories.

These recipes are not always traditional, I've adopted and adapted them from friends, or taught myself. I highly suggest you ask your friends about their origins and traditions: it's exciting, and a beautiful way to deepen your relationships by sharing and learning from each other.

I sincerely hope you see this book as a marker of cultural appreciation rather than appropriation and that it will inspire you to ask questions and explore diverse and unique tastes, flavours, scents, textures and more. I have had the privilege of learning about different cultures, expanding my worldwide knowledge through feedback from so many of you. I am so lucky to be learning daily about the world from the comfort of my kitchen, through tips and tricks sent over to me from kind readers, watchers and friends. There is still so much to taste and learn, so it's never too late to get started!

Acknowledgements

Never in my life did I think this would be the hardest part of the book to write. I have been surrounded by the most wonderful people during this entire experience who not only believed in me, but also championed my crazy world of condiments. Thank you so much for supporting me, pushing me and allowing me this opportunity.

My dream agent Kate, thank you for reading hundreds of pages on the history of chili/chilli/chile. I so appreciate your guidance during this new chapter of mine and I sincerely have never trusted anyone in the workplace as much as you. I hope you're ready for the non-stop text messages to continue with book two because you're never getting rid of me!

To the lovely team at Bloomsbury, thank you so much. You've given me the opportunity of a lifetime and made the process so enjoyable. Grace and Lena, on our first meeting, I knew that if I could publish this book with anyone, it would be with you. Your curiosity, insight and excitement about my words pushed me and your clear directions kept me calm, focused and inspired. I am so grateful that we were able to embark on this journey together. And Lucy, I still don't know how you do it! Your meticulous editing made me feel so safe in the final stages of the book.

To the Evi O team, thank you so much for bringing my vision to life and understanding what I meant when I said I wanted the book to look '*happy*'. Eloise, your watercolours are unmatched and your willingness to change a line on a doodle to match my vision is frankly commendable. May this be the first of many projects together.

I am still in shock that I was able to work with such a talented group of women and for that I am eternally thankful. I will miss our lovey-dovey, 7am video calls very much.

To my friends, I am so grateful for your patience with me during this time and for always being up for a taste test. Nicola, I genuinely don't know how I could've written this book without you. I am so lucky to call one of my best friends my inspiration. Kathryn, I'm so glad the internet thinks we're dating: you're better than any man out there. Izzy, text me back. Grazie, thank you for forcing me out of the kitchen for a very-needed glass of champagne and lots of laughter. Shuku and Avni, thank you for being my designated spicy taste-testers. Lia, thank you for helping me bring my original Stinkometer to life. Yassy, thank you for being the sister I never had *#chefdidierforever*. And lastly, Amanda, thank you for telling me to post an Instagram story of all of the condiments in my fridge that day... you unknowingly changed the trajectory of my life and to you I am eternally grateful.

To my history teachers, thank you for propelling my love of learning. Whether you were one of the many who encouraged me to go ahead and learn about the history of a niche subject, or one of the few that most certainly did not, this book is all thanks to you. A special shoutout goes to Jonathan Stamp, who initiated my love of history at the young age of six. Thank you for your storytelling and for walking me down the streets of ancient Rome. Lastly, I want to thank the one and only Sally Shultz from the brown chair for teaching me proper English grammar when my French accent was still in full swing.

To my jolly neighbourhood, thank you for being the community I never knew I needed. My morning strolls in the fresh London drizzle kept me sane and saying hello to all my neighbours kept me grounded, motivated and happy during the entire process.

Finally, *un grand merci à ma petite famille. Maman, Papa (Tomate et la dame de Haute Savoie), je ne sais pas où je serais sans vous. Je vous aime à l'infini. Merci d'avoir toujours cru en moi et de m'avoir laissée manger des anchois et de l'ail à deux mois.* And last but most certainly not least, I want to thank my Lali for introducing me to food from a culture other than my own and for teaching me that family has nothing to do with blood. *¡Te quiero muchísimo!*

S

U

V

W

Y

BLOOMSBURY PUBLISHING

Bloomsbury Publishing Plc

50 Bedford Square, London, WC1B 3DP, UK

29 Earlsfort Terrace, Dublin 2, Ireland

BLOOMSBURY, BLOOMSBURY PUBLISHING and the Diana logo are trademarks of Bloomsbury Publishing Plc

First published in Great Britain 2024

A catalogue record for this book is available from the British Library.

ISBN: HB 978-1-5266-6978-0;
eBook: 978-1-5266-6979-7;
Audio: 978-1-5266-6981-0

2 4 6 8 10 9 7 5 3 1

Project Editor Lucy Bannell

Designer Evi-O. Studio | Evi O., Eloise Myatt

Illustrator Evi-O. Studio | Eloise Myatt, Siena Zadro and Katherine Zhang

Indexer Vanessa Bird

Printed and bound in Dubai by Oriental Press

To find out more about our authors and books visit www.bloomsbury.com and sign up for our newsletters.

GOUDA 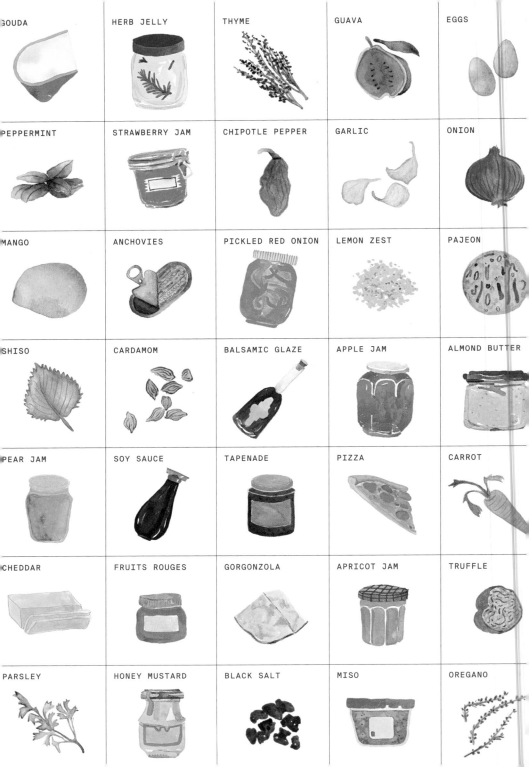	HERB JELLY	THYME	GUAVA	EGGS
PEPPERMINT	STRAWBERRY JAM	CHIPOTLE PEPPER	GARLIC	ONION
MANGO	ANCHOVIES	PICKLED RED ONION	LEMON ZEST	PAJEON
SHISO	CARDAMOM	BALSAMIC GLAZE	APPLE JAM	ALMOND BUTTER
PEAR JAM	SOY SAUCE	TAPENADE	PIZZA	CARROT
CHEDDAR	FRUITS ROUGES	GORGONZOLA	APRICOT JAM	TRUFFLE
PARSLEY	HONEY MUSTARD	BLACK SALT	MISO	OREGANO